The Structure of Hebrews

Biblical Studies Library

The Descent of Christ: Ephesians 4:7–11 and Traditional Hebrew Imagery, W. Hall Harris III

Marriage as a Covenant: Biblical Law and Ethics as Developed from Malachi, Gordon P. Hugenberger

The Structure of Hebrews: A Text-Linguistic Analysis, George H. Guthrie

The Structure of Hebrews

A Text-Linguistic Analysis

George H. Guthrie

Baker Books

A Division of Baker Book House Co
Grand Rapids, Michigan 49516

© 1994 by E. J. Brill, Leiden, The Netherlands

Published by Baker Books
a division of Baker Book House Company
P.O. Box 6287, Grand Rapids, MI 49516-6287

First cloth edition published 1994 by E. J. Brill as volume 73 in Supplements to Novum Testamentum.

First paperback edition published 1998 by Baker Books.

Printed in the United States of America

Library of Congress Cataloging-in-Publication Data

Guthrie, George H.
    The structure of Hebrews : a text-linguistic analysis / George H. Guthrie.
       p.   cm. — (Biblical studies library)
    Originally published: Leiden, The Netherlands ; New York : E. J. Brill, 1994, in series: Supplements to Novum Testamentum; v. 73.
    Includes bibliographical references and index.
    ISBN 0-8010-2193-6 (pbk.)
    1. Bible. N.T. Hebrews–Criticism, interpretation, etc.
    I. Title. II. Series.
    [BS2775.2.G887   1998]
    227'.87066–DC21   98-38641

For information about academic books, resources for Christian leaders, and all new releases available from Baker Book House, visit our web site:
http://www.bakerbooks.com

To Pat

TABLE OF CONTENTS

PART I

PAST PROPOSALS ON THE STRUCTURE OF HEBREWS

PART II

TEXT-LINGUISTIC ANALYSIS OF THE
STRUCTURE OF HEBREWS

PREFACE

Most people think that reading a text largely requires a knowledge of the alphabet, the grammar and, especially, the meaning of a sizeable number of the words of a particular language. It usually comes as a surprise to learn that although these skills as such are imperative to the competence of reading a text, they so often leave the reader without a proper understanding of what a text really communicates. The matter becomes more complex when linguists insist that the 'meanings' of words are often misunderstood by many readers for not recognizing the difference between the lexical meanings of words and their contextual usages. The worst comes when linguists also insist that there are different levels of meaning: word meaning, phrase meaning, sentence meaning, and discourse meaning. Therefore, understanding a text is more than reading 'just as it stands,' since the meaning of a sentence is not merely the sum of the meanings of the words comprising the sentence. Similarly, discourses are not a matter of sentences strung together.

Reading is, in fact, a very complex process—and more so for ancient texts. It is precisely here where discourse analysis reveals how a text is read. It also reveals that such a reading is not necessarily a final reading, but rather a demonstration, a giving account, of how a text is taken apart for its various layers to be seen and appreciated—and how it is then again put together with proper demarcation of its understood intent. In other words, it shows how and what a reader compares or contrasts in recognizing the various semantic units of a text that are utilized in putting together the argument developed in a text. To a certain extent any competent reader of any text applies, even subconsciously, a sizeable number of semantic features derived from the text in order to come to an understanding of what the text communicates. This is why even scholarly commentaries on complicated texts may differ to various degrees. It is finally, to a large extent, due to one's comprehension of the structure of the text.

The Epistle to the Hebrews is known to have challenged scholars for some time with the problem of its overall structure. For the last thirty years, in particular, many have attempted to join Albert

Vanhoye who introduced the problem of the structure of the Epistle
as crucial to understanding its message. Quite dissimilar approaches
were presented. They had, however, one feature in common. They
all assumed that the Epistle had a linear structure. Gradually the
impression grew that Hebrews was perhaps not that well structured
originally.

When I received the manuscript my first reaction was that this
might be yet another of the many relatively futile attempts to un-
ravel the strange flow of the argument in Hebrews. However, this
proved not to be the case. The proposed structure presented here
introduces a new feature to discourse analysis in that it opens the
way for recognizing that careful text linguistics need not reveal only
a linear division of connected units that eventually may reveal some
overall pattern, but that a discourse can have divisions that run, as
it were, simultaneously. Two major semantic discourse notions defined as expository and hortatory respectively, are proposed. These
two notions can be separately considered since the author of the
Epistle shifts back and forth between exposition and exhortation.
The structure of Hebrews can, therefore, best be seen if these are
first taken apart and set forth by reflecting the point by point argument in each unit. In this way one can then see that the complex
structure of Hebrews is due to two notions or genres moving in
concert along their own lines but progressing towards the same goal
of challenging the readers/hearers to endure.

Whether New Testament scholarship will accept this solution of a
dual discourse structure, that is, of almost two discourses interwo-
ven, is no excuse for not taking notice of this proposal which is in
itself a helpful departure from previous attempts. The reading of
Hebrews proposed in this book is not only important for understanding the structure of the Epistle, but is also notable for the
discipline of discourse analysis itself. It is surely a well argued new
approach worthy to be taken seriously and contributing to a fresh
reading of Hebrews.

Johannes P. Louw
University of Pretoria

ACKNOWLEDGEMENTS

The present volume represents a step in my own study of the book of Hebrews. Hopefully the fruit here will continue to ripen in coming years, but it would have certainly been stunted or died on the vine without a network of encouragers who have contributed to my growth and work. I gratefully take this opportunity to recognize the community of friends and mentors who have contributed to its development.

Drs. Grant Osborne and Walter Liefeld, readers of my Master's thesis at Trinity Evangelical Divinity School, initially encouraged me to develop my embryonic work on the structure of Hebrews. Dr. Bruce Corley, Dean of the School of Theology at Southwestern Seminary and my supervisor on the doctoral dissertation, not only fulfilled his role with grace and skill but continues to be a stimulating partner in dialogue concerning Hebrews. I look forward to many more sessions for which we never seem to have enough time. Two other professors at Southwestern, Dr. Thomas Lea and Dr. E. Earle Ellis, graciously read the manuscript in dissertation form and offered helpful suggestions.

At the eleventh hour of his work on volumes for the Word Biblical Commentary Series, Dr. William Lane opened himself to both serious dialogue on the structure of Hebrews and a mentoring relationship. His encouragement and insights are second in value only to our continuing friendship. I also appreciate the exposure his introduction has already afforded my research.

Although our time was brief, I benefitted from discussion with Dr. Walter Übelacker at the 1992 national S.B.L. meeting in San Francisco. Dr. Übelacker has provided the scholarly community with an excellent rhetorical analysis of Hebrews, and I expect to continue to learn from him in years to come.

My colleague Dr. J. Scott Duvall provided a welcomed sounding board from the earliest stages of the work and proved a friend genuinely interested in my spiritual and emotional wellbeing. Dr. Louise Bentley graciously offered her service of editing the manuscript in the midst of a terribly hectic schedule. Her aid in the areas of wording and punctuation has been felt throughout the volume.

I am also grateful to the administration, my colleagues, the librarians, and my students at Union University for their encouragement and the provision of an atmosphere conducive to intellectual growth and dialogue.

Dr. Carey Newman, who has an earlier volume in this series, initially encouraged Brill to consider my work. Thanks to Hans van der Meij, the acquisitions editor for Brill, and the series editors for the opportunity to get the work before the Academy. Also, thanks to J. P. Louw for his evaluation of my work and for consenting to write the preface to the book.

Finally, and most importantly, I acknowledge the multiple roles of my wife Pat. She has been a partner in every sense of the word, providing love, friendship, a dinner and dialogue partner, prayers, compassion, encouragement, and insight on my research and writing. She has helped savor the joys of success and offered exhortation to get on with the process!

To all these I offer thanks. To God alone be glory.

George H. Guthrie
July 1993

LIST OF ILLUSTRATIONS

INTRODUCTION

Since the publication of Albert Vanhoye's monograph *La structure littéraire de l'Épître aux Hébreux* in 1963, debate over the structure of Hebrews has elevated to a noticeable, if not fevered, pitch—and for good reason.[1] Even a casual perusal of recently published commentaries on Hebrews demonstrates the vast disparity between current approaches to the book's organization of material. Almost as many outlines are set forth as there are scholars who take up the task.

Yet this apparent confusion is nothing new. Inquiries into the structure of this distinctively complex work have been going on for centuries. As in the current debate, those inquiries have often followed disparate paths in both their methodologies and conclusions.

The question presents itself: if a scholar is confused, uncertain, or incorrect in evaluating the structure of an author's discourse, is that scholar not destined to flounder at points when presenting propositions concerning the author's intended meanings in the various sections of that discourse? Stated another way, can accurate exegesis of a given passage be carried out without a proper understanding of the broader literary context in which that passage is found? Certainly an accurate assessment of a book's structure is vital for an accurate assessment of that book's meaning. Therefore, questions

---

[1] Albert Vanhoye, *La structure littéraire de l'Épître aux Hébreux*, 2d ed. (Lyon: Desclée de Brouwer, 1976). For introductions to discussions on the structure of Hebrews see ibid., 16-32; William L. Lane, *Hebrews 1-8*, Word Biblical Commentary (Dallas, TX: Word, 1991), lxxv-xcviii; Otto Michel, *Der Brief an die Hebräer*, Kritisch-exegetischer Kommentar über das Neue Testament Begründet von Heinrich August Wilhelm Meyer (Göttingen: Vandenhoeck & Ruprecht, 1966), 29-35; Harold Attridge, *To the Hebrews*, Hermeneia (Philadelphia: Fortress Press, 1989), 14-21; Helmut Feld, *Der Hebräerbrief Erträge der Forschung* (Darmstadt: Wissenschaftliche Buchgesel, 1985), 23-29; Ceslas Spicq, *L'Épître aux Hébreux*, 1 (Paris: J. Gabalda, 1952-53), 27-38; David Alan Black, "The Problem of the Literary Structure of Hebrews: An Evaluation and a Proposal," *Grace Theological Journal* 7 (1986): 163-77; J. C. McCullough, "Some Recent Developments in Research on the Epistle to the Hebrews," *Irish Biblical Studies* 3 (1980): 153-56; Walter G. Übelacker, *Der Hebräerbrief als Appell: Untersuchungen zu exordium, narratio und postscriptum (Hebr 1-2 und 13, 22-25)*, Coniectanea Biblica, New Testament Series (Lund: Almqvist & Wiksell International, 1989): 11-48.

concerning the structure of Hebrews are important for understanding the message of the book.

This study offers an attempt at assessing the structure of Hebrews with the hope that the book's message will be further clarified. Part I identifies past proposals on that structure and consists of two chapters. Chapter 1 sets forth a brief history of speculations on the topic. Works are presented as either representative of the age in which they were produced or as unique contributions to the unfolding history of investigation. In Chapter 2 the study analyzes various positions in the current debate. The chapter commences with consideration of proposed outlines in order to highlight the great disparity between current assessments of the book's structure. However, the balance of the chapter focuses on methodologies used to analyze Hebrews. These methodologies are categorized and assessed for both their strengths and weaknesses.

Part II moves the study to an examination of the text of Hebrews itself and consists of five chapters. Chapter 3 presents the methodology used in the present investigation. Although highly eclectic, the method has the most affinity with modern text linguistics, a branch of linguistics which seeks to understand the interplay of units of text in a discourse. The text-linguistic analysis here, however, seeks to be ever sensitive to literary and oratorical conventions of the first century.

Chapters 4 through 7 embody a critical analysis of the structure of Hebrews. Chapter 4 and the greater part of Chapter 5 focus on the isolation of individual units via identification of unit boundaries. From the end of Chapter 5 through Chapter 6 the aim is to set forth various means of interrelationship between units in Hebrews. The study arrives at its ultimate purpose in Chapter 7 with the logic behind the arrangement of those units clarified.

Hebrews stands as a praiseworthy example of ancient homiletic craftsmanship, an example which in all its complexity exhibits rhetorical power and beauty.[2] The author's craft, however, may seem

---

[2] For work on Hebrews as a sermon see Erich Grässer, "Der Hebräerbrief 1938-1963," *Theologische Rundschau* 30 (1964): 159-60; George B. Caird, "The Exegetical Method of the Epistle to the Hebrews," *Canadian Journal of Theology* 5 (1959): 44-51; H. Zimmermann, *Das Bekenntnis der Hoffnung: Tradition und Redaktion im Hebräerbrief* (Köln: Peter Hanstein Verlag, 1977), 5-8; Hartwig Thyen, *Der Stil des jüdisch-hellenistischen Homilie* (Göttingen: Vandenhoeck & Ruprecht, 1955); Werner

opaque to moderns unfamiliar with his conventions. Those conventions, therefore, must be investigated to understand the twists and turns of this complex work. May the present study serve their elucidation, and in so doing, the clarification of this "word of exhortation."

Georg Kümmel, *Introduction to the New Testament*, trans. Howard Clark Kee (Nashville: Abingdon, 1975), 398; William L. Lane, "Hebrews: A Sermon in Search of a Setting," *Southwestern Journal of Theology* 28 (1985): 13-18.

PART ONE

PAST PROPOSALS ON THE STRUCTURE OF HEBREWS

CHAPTER ONE

HISTORY OF INVESTIGATION

Earliest Attempts

The *kephalaia*, a system of chapter divisions used in the ancient Greek manuscripts, is the earliest extant witness to formal divisions in the text of Hebrews.[1] According to this system, Hebrews was divided into twenty-two sections (corresponding to modern chapter and verse divisions) at 1:5, 2:9, 3:1, 4:1, 4:11, 5:11, 6:13, 7:1, 7:11, 8:7, 9:11, 10:5, 10:24, 10:32, 11:1, 12:1, 12:12, 12:18, 13:1, 13:9, and 13:20. The rationale behind these divisions seems to be a turn in the author's discussion most often marked by a conjunction.[2] Seventeen times the beginning of a new section corresponds to a paragraph division in the Nestle-Aland text, and six correspond to the beginning of a new chapter as designated in the modern era.

Rather than utilizing formal divisions, however, earliest commentators simply included an overview of the author's argument in either their introductions or expositions. For example, at the beginning of his exposition on Hebrews 7 the fourth century preacher John Chrysostom provided a brief review of chapters 1-6 and commented on their role in preparing the way for the discussion which follows.[3] Similarly, in his *Argumentum* (i.e., introduction) on Hebrews, Theodoret set forth a broad overview of the book, primarily emphasizing Christ's superiority over various Old Testament institutions.[4]

---

[1] Eberhard Nestle and Erwin Nestle, *Novum Testamentum Graece*, 26th ed., ed. Kurt Aland and others (Stuttgart: Deutsche Bibelgesellschaft, 1979), 35, 69.

[2] The most common conjunctions appearing at the beginning of *kephalaia* sections are γάρ and δέ, each appearing five times. Other conjunctions or particles used are οὖν, διό, καί, τοιγαροῦν, and ὅθεν. None appear at 5:11, 13:1, and 13:9.

[3] John Chrysostom, "OMIΛIA IB´," in J.-P. Mingne, ed., *Patrologia Graeca*, 63 (Paris, 1862), 423.

[4] Theodoret, "Commentarius in omnes sancti Pauli Epistolas," in J.-P. Migne, ed., *Patrologia Graeca*, 82 (Paris, 1862), 677-78.

MEDIEVAL AND REFORMATION PERIODS

It probably was not until the thirteenth century that chapter and verse divisions were introduced to the text and thus became available for denoting apportionments of the book of Hebrews.[5] One of the earliest assessments of Hebrews utilizing chapter and verse divisions was that of Thomas Aquinas, who, with Theodoret, focused on the *excellentiam Christi* theme. Aquinas' evaluation broke the book into two main divisions, the first on the superiority of Christ (chaps. 1-10) and the second on how members should join the leader (chaps. 11-13). Aquinas subdivided the first division into three movements: Christ's superiority over the angels (chaps. 1-2), over Moses (chaps. 3-4), and over the Old Testament priesthood (chaps. 5-10). He subdivided the second main division into two parts: members should join the leader by faith (chap. 11) and by works of faith (chaps. 12-13).[6]

As was the case with Aquinas, in the *Argumenta* of works produced during the medieval and reformation periods, authors provided a summary of the contents of the book in paragraph form. Most commented on the contents chapter by chapter and understood Hebrews to center around the doctrine of Christ's superiority.[7]

There were, however, notable exceptions. Heinrich Bullinger divided the book into a tripartite scheme, sections one (chaps. 1-4) and three (10:19-13) being each a *deliberativum*, or firm exhortation, and section two (5:1-10:18) a *didacticum* on Christ as the true priest. Note that Bullinger saw a break in the middle of chapter 10, thus departing from grouping the contents of the book by chapter divisions. He further identified the author's method of argumentation

---

[5] F. F. Bruce, *The Books and the Parchments: How We Got Our English Bible*, rev. and updated ed. (Old Tappan, NJ: Fleming H. Revell, 1984), 112.

[6] Thomas Aquinas, *In Omnes S. Pauli Apostoli Epistolas Commentaria*, 2 (Taurini: Petri Marietti, 1924), 288.

[7] Kenneth Hagen, *Hebrews Commenting from Erasmus to Bèze 1516-1598*, Beiträge zur Geschichte der Biblischen Exegese (Tübingen: J. C. B. Mohr [Paul Siebeck], 1981), 8; Spicq, *L'Épître aux Hébreux*, 28. E.g., H. Zwingli and John Calvin both build their expositions of the book around this commonly cited motif. See H. Zwingli, *In evangelicam historicam de domino nostro Iesu Christo, per Matthaeum, Marcum, Lucam, et Joannem conscriptam, epistolas que aliquot Pauli, annotationes D. Huldrychi Zwingli per Leonem Iudae exceptae et aeditae. Adjecta est epistola Pauli ad Hebraeos, et Joannis Apostoli epistola per Gasparem Megandrum* (Zürich: Christoph Froschouer, 1539); John Calvin, *Commentaries on the Epistle to the Hebrews*, trans. John Owen (Grand Rapids, MI: Wm. B. Eerdmans, 1949), xxviii-xxix.

in the book as *maior et melior*, a procedure common in rabbinical exegesis of the first century.[8]

Another commentator who broke from the norm was Niels Hemmingsen. In a section entitled *Ordo, seu Tractationis Methodus*, Hemmingsen suggested the author of Hebrews unraveled his discourse on the basis of ancient rhetorical practice. He saw the first section as a *narratio* on the person and office of the Son of God. This was then followed by a well-crafted exhortation for the hearers to pay close attention to the message. Having heightened their attention, the author embarked on a *disputatio* concerning the priesthood of Christ. He closed by giving examples of faith and basic principles for living.[9] The rhetorical approach of Hemmingsen, Bullinger's tripartite scheme, as well as the more common thematic method of tracking the κρείττων motif throughout Hebrews, would be championed into the modern era.

EIGHTEENTH AND NINETEENTH CENTURIES

During the eighteenth century John Albert Bengel proposed fresh suggestions on the structure of Hebrews in his *Gnomon*.[10] Based on a rigorous exegesis of the text, Bengel's outline divided the book into two primary movements. This bipartite division was vastly different from earlier bipartite schemes (e.g., Aquinas) which primarily divided the book between chapters 10 and 11.

As demonstrated in fig. 1, Bengel understood 1:1-2:4 to be an introduction on Christ's superiority and the need to listen to his superior word. He believed 2:1-4 to be the hortatory climax which built on the exposition in chapter 1. Bengel further suggested an integral relationship between 2:5-18, on Christ becoming lower than the angels (playing off of Ps. 8:5-9), and the balance of Hebrews on Christ's priesthood. He essentially understood the author's

---

[8] Heinrich Bullinger, *In Piam et Eruditam Pauli ad Hebraeos Epistolam, Heinrychi Bullingeri Commentarius* (Zürich: Christoph Froschouer, 1532), 490-91; trans. Kenneth Hagen, *Hebrews Commenting from Erasmus to Bèza 1516-1598*, 24-26.

[9] Niels Hemmingsen, *Commentaria in omnes Epistolas Apostolorum, Pauli, Petri, Iudae, Ioannis, Iacobi, et in eam quae ad Hebraeos inscribitur* (Frankfurt: Georg Corvinus, 1579), 831; quoted in Kenneth Hagen, *Hebrews Commenting from Erasmus to Bèza 1516-1598*, 80-81.

[10] John Albert Bengel, *Gnomon of the New Testament*, trans. James Bryce, 6th ed. (Edinburgh: T. & T. Clark, 1866), 335.

  I. From a previous comparison with the Prophets and Angels (1:1-14)
       Therefore we ought to give heed to what He says (2:1-4)
 II. [His glory shines forth] principally from a comparison of His suffering
       and His consummation. We must here observe
      1. The proposition and sum from Ps. 8:5-9
      2. The discussion: We have the Author of salvation and glory per-
          fected [consummated]; who suffered first for our sakes, that He
          might become (1) a merciful, and (2) Faithful (3) High Priest
          (2:10-18). These three things are one by one explained, being
          most suitably from time to time interwoven with His passion and
          His consummation.
    A. He has the virtues of priesthood:
      1. He is Faithful:
          Therefore be ye not unfaithful (3:1,2,7-4:13)
      2. He is Merciful:
          Therefore let us draw near with confidence (4:14-5:3)
    B. He is called of God a Priest. Here—
      1. The sum (of His priesthood) is set forth from Ps. 2 and 110,
          and from His actual performance of the duties of the office
          (5:4-10); And hence the hearers are summarily roused to
          action (5:11-6:20)
      2. The fact itself is copiously
        (1) Explained. He is to us:
           α. A Great High Priest
              1. Such as Ps. 110 describes
                  1) According to the order of
                      Melchizedek (7:1-19)
                  2) With an oath (7:20-22)
                  3) forever (7:23,24,26-28)
              2. And therefore particularly excellent
                  1) a heavenly priest (8:1-6)
                  2) and that of the New Covenant
                      (8:7-13)
           β. The Entrance into the Sanctuary (9:1-10:18)
        (2) It is turned to a practical exhortation.
           Therefore
           1. Evince your faith, hope, love (10:19-13:6)
           2. For improvement in these graces, call to re-
               membrance your former ministers
               (13:7-16) And make use of the watchfulness of
               your present ministers (13:17-19)
Doxology and calm conclusion (13:20-25) [italics mine]

Fig. 1. Bengel's outline of Hebrews.

argument to be that the incarnation (2:5-18) prepared the way for Christ's appointment and ministry as High Priest.

Bengel's outline, although cumbersome, contains characteristics which provide insights into the structure of Hebrews. First, he highlighted the author's use of exhortation, demonstrating both its unique function in the discourse and its dependence on the expositional material. Hortatory passages are set apart and introduced with "Therefore."

Second, Bengel underscored use of Old Testament texts in development of the author's discussion, especially Psalms 2, 8, and 110. He noted that these, on several occasions, form a point of departure for the author's discussion. They are, therefore, functionally pivotal in the author's argument.[11]

Finally, the function of three words at the end of chapter 2— "faithful," "merciful," and "high priest"—were cited by Bengel as being key words upon which the author would build the arguments which followed. This insight, not related to Bengel, would form a foundation stone upon which one twentieth-century stream of thought on the book's structure would be developed.[12]

No true advances were forthcoming in the nineteenth century, most scholars basing their assessments on detailed exegesis of the text and organizing the book around the author's development of assorted themes. Commentators variously presented their understanding of the book's configuration in paragraph form in the introduction,[13] in an outline in the introduction,[14] or in a table of

---

[11] This point has failed to receive adequate consideration in current studies on the structure of Hebrews. It will be demonstrated below that a proper understanding of the uses of the Old Testament in Hebrews is of fundamental importance for understanding the structure of the book.

[12] It seems that stream of thought, grounded in the work of F. Thien and carried through by Leon Vaganay and Albert Vanhoye, developed independently of Bengel's work. See infra, 11-17.

[13] E.g., Bernard Weiss, *Kritisch Exegetisches Handbuch über den Brief an die Hebräer*, Kritisch Exegetischer Kommentar über das Neue Testament (Göttingen: Vandenhoeck und Ruprecht's, 1888), 34; Moses Stuart, *A Commentary on the Epistle to the Hebrews* (repr., London: Fisher, Son, & Co., 1833), 243-48. Gottlieb Lünemann, in his introduction, divided Hebrews according to the author's development of his discourse, yet the commentary itself is laid out chapter by chapter. See Gottlieb Lünemann, *Critical and Exegetical Handbook to the Epistle to the Hebrews*, trans. Maurice J. Evans, Critical and Exegetical Commentary on the New Testament (Edinburgh: T. & T. Clark, 1882), 57-62.

[14] E.g., Frederic Rendall, *The Epistle to the Hebrews* (London: MacMillan and Co., 1888), 1-6; Carl Bernhard Moll, *The Epistle to the Hebrews*, trans. Philip Schaff, Commentary on the Holy Scriptures (New York: Charles Scribner's Sons, 1887), 20-21.

contents.[15] Others abstained from remarks on the structure alto-
gether.

Methodologically, Hermann F. von Soden presented not only a
thematic arrangement of Hebrews, but also analyzed the construction of Hebrews along the lines of classical Greek rhetoric.[16] In his
commentary on Hebrews von Soden suggested a four-part scheme
involving a προοίμιον with a presentation of the πρόθεσις (Heb.
1-4), διήγησις πρός πιθανότητα (5-6), ἀπόδειξις πρός πειθώ (7:1-
10:18), and ἐπίλογος (10:19-13).[17] He would later be followed, with
slight revisions, by Theodore Haering and Hans Windisch.[18]

THE TWENTIETH CENTURY

As in prior centuries, discussions on the structure of Hebrews in the
twentieth century have traversed diverse methodological paths, set
forth various suggestions as to the organizational principle behind
the book, and arrived at a plethora of outlines. Although some
scholars continue to utilize methods of past centuries, new methodologies accompanied by new proposals have appeared. Introductory remarks concerning the structure of Hebrews have been joined
by debate in the present, scholars commenting on the proposals of
other scholars. Three streams of discussion have brought especially
fresh insights to the debate: (1) "Genre Differentiation" as carried
out by F. Büchsel and Rafael Gyllenberg, (2) the "Literary Analysis" of Leon Vaganay, Albert Vanhoye, and others, and (3) the
tripartite scheme advanced especially by Wolfgang Nauck.

---

[15] E.g., Franz Delitzsch, *Commentary on the Epistle to the Hebrews*, trans. Thomas L.
Kingsbury (Edinburgh: T. & T. Clark, 1878), v-vii.

[16] Hermann Frhr. von Soden, *Urchristliche Literaturgeschichte: die Schriften des Neuen
Testaments* (Berlin: Alexander Duncker, 1905), 127-28.

[17] Idem, *Der Brief an die Hebräer*, in *Hebräerbrief, Briefe des Petrus, Jakobus, Judas*, 2,
3d ed., Hand-Commentar zum Neue Testament (Tübingen: J. C. B. Mohr [Paul
Siebeck],1899), 8-11.

[18] Theodore Haering, "Gedankengang und Grundgedanken des Hebräerbriefs," *Zeitschrift für die Neutestamentliche Wissenschaft* 18 (1917-18): 153; Hans Windisch, *Der Hebräerbrief, Handbuch zum Neuen Testament* (Tübingen: J. C. B. Mohr
[Paul Siebeck], 1931), 8.

Büchsel, Gyllenberg, and Genre
Differentiation

F. Büchsel

In 1928 F. Büchsel set forth a proposal concerning the structure of Hebrews based on the author's back and forth switch between exposition and exhortation, the two dominant genres in the book.[19] According to Büchsel the interplay between these genres marks five movements in Hebrews. In all but the second, expositional material is followed by exhortation, as demonstrated in fig. 2.

I.	*exposition:* 1:1-14	*exhortation:* 2:1-4
II.	*exposition:* 2:5-18	[none]
III.	*exposition:* 3:1-6	*exhortation:* 3:7-4:13
IV.	*exposition:* 4:14-10:18	*exhortation:* 10:19-39
V.	*exposition:* 11:1-40	*exhortation:* 12:1-29

Fig. 2. Büchsel's outline of Hebrews, highlighting genre switching between exposition and exhortation.

Büchsel understood Hebrews 13 to be a single admonition with an epistolary ending.

Rafael Gyllenberg

Approximately thirty years later Rafael Gyllenberg would follow and modify Büchsel's proposal in his article entitled, "Die Komposition des Hebräerbriefs."[20] Gyllenberg also composed five sections, as fig. 3 demonstrates. He departed from Büchsel by combining Büchsel's sections I and II and extending the exhortation in chapter 4 through 4:16. Accordingly, section III (Büchsel's fourth section) then began with 5:1. Furthermore, Gyllenberg made 10:19-12:29 his section IV, and chapter 13 became section V. In his outline Gyllenberg italicized the hortatory subdivisions, pointing out the correspondence between sections I and III and sections II and IV.

---

[19] Hermann Gunkel and Leopold Zscharnack, eds., *Religion in Geschichte und Gegenwart: Handwörterbuch für Theologie und Religionswissenschaft*, 2d ed. (Tübingen: J. C. B. Mohr [Paul Siebeck], 1928), s.v. "Hebräerbrief," by F. Büchsel. As discussed above, J. A. Bengel highlighted the use of hortatory material in Hebrews. For Büchsel and Gyllenberg, however, the switch between genres constituted the primary organizational principle behind the book.

[20] Rafael Gyllenberg, "Die Komposition des Hebräerbriefs," *Svensk Exegetisk Årsbok* 22-23 (1957-1958): 137-47.

I.	Christ as Our Guide to Salvation	1,1-2,18
A	The Definitive Revealer	1,1-4
B	The Enthronement of the Revealer	1,1-14
C	*Invitation to Receive the Revelation*	2,1-4
D	Incarnation and Conquest of the Revealer	2,5-18
II.	The Wandering People of God	3,1-4,16
A	*Christ Superior to Moses*	3,1-6
B	*The Imitation of Christ*	3,7-4,13
C	*The Confidence to Achieve Salvation*	4,14-16
III.	Christ as Our High Priest	5,1-10,18
A	Christ as Our High Priest According to the Old System	5,1-10
B	*The Spiritual Backwardness of the Reader*	5,11-6,20
C	Christ as Our High Priest According to the Order of Melchizedek	7,1-28
D	Christ as the Heavenly High Priest	8,1-10,18
IV.	The Church's Way of Faith	10,19-12,29
A	*The Trip of the Heavenly Glory Approaches*	10,19-39
B	*The Faith and Its Witnesses*	11,1-40
C	*The Continual Trip in Persistent Faith*	12,1-29
V.	Final Exhortation and Conclusion	13,1-25

Fig. 3. Gyllenberg's outline of Hebrews.[21]

Weaknesses appear in the structural assessments offered by both Büchsel and Gyllenberg. In recent discussions the exact role of hortatory against expository material in Hebrews has become an issue of heated debate, some suggesting that to hold the two apart is to damage the integrity of the book. Nevertheless, Büchsel and Gyllenberg advanced discussion on the structure of Hebrews by highlighting these two distinct genres which dominate the major portions of the book. The rationale behind their proposals lies in the distinctiveness of the two genres, to be explored in the present study.[22]

[21] Ibid., 145-46.

[22] Gyllenberg observed that, unlike the expository material, exhortation in the book appears to return again and again to a similar theme. Ibid., 139-40.

The Vaganay-Vanhoye School

F. Thien

In *Revue Biblique* at the turn of the century F. Thien set forth proposals which have proven vastly influential in the latter half of the twentieth century, some affecting outlines on Hebrews to the present.[23] Thien observed most commentaries divided the book into two main parts: 1:1-10:18 and 10:19-13:25. His aim was to offer new divisions of the book based on insight concerning how the author organized his material.[24]

Thien suggested the center section of Hebrews, or the *"Corpus Orationis,"* is made up of three major movements (3:1-5:10, 7:1-10:39, and 11:1-12:29), each of which has two primary themes. He noticed that these themes are "announced" just prior to the beginning of the unit in which they are developed and then discussed in *inverse* order. For example, at the end of Hebrews chapter 2 Jesus is called the *merciful* and *faithful* High Priest. The author then, according to Thien, discusses Jesus as "faithful" in 3:1-4:13 and Jesus as "merciful" in 4:14-5:10.[25]

This process is repeated in the next section. In 5:9-10 Jesus is called the *source of eternal salvation* and *a priest according to the order of Melchizedek*. Following a hortatory introduction (5:11-6:20), the author deals first with "Jesus, a priest according to the order of Melchizedek" (chap. 7) and then, "Jesus, source of our salvation" (8:1-10:18). The final section deals with examples of faith (chap. 11) and faith's practical consequences (chap. 12), themes which are announced at the end of chapter 10.[26] Thien considered Hebrews 1 and 2 the introduction to the book with Hebrews 13 the conclusion.

Leon Vaganay

Thien's proposals were followed and developed by Leon Vaganay, whose article, "Le Plan de L'Épître aux Hébreux," may be considered the beginning of modern literary discussions on the structure

---

[23] F. Thien, "Analyse de L'Épître aux Hébreux," *Revue Biblique* 11 (1902): 74-86. Thien has influenced more recent scholars through the work of Leon Vaganay and Albert Vanhoye. For those who have followed Vaganay and Vanhoye see *infra*, 13,16.

[24] Ibid., 74-75.

[25] Ibid., 80-81; cf. the proposal of J. A. Bengel, *supra*, 5-7.

[26] Ibid., 82-85.

of Hebrews.[27] Vaganay observed that while all critics had recognized the literary quality of Hebrews, even those few who had personally studied rhetorical aspects of the work had been forced to admit that they did not clearly understand its distribution of material.[28] Although obviously influenced by Thien's broad outline of the book, as shown in fig. 4, Vaganay moved beyond Thien on at least two primary fronts.

Most importantly, he advanced discussion on the structure of Hebrews with his identification of *mot-crochets*, "hook words," in the book. Hook words were a rhetorical device used in the ancient world to tie two sections of material together. A word was positioned at the end of one section and at the beginning of the next to effect a transition between the two.[29]

For example, at the end of Heb. 1:1-4 (the introduction according to Vaganay) the author refers to τῶν ἀγγέλων. He then "hooks" the introduction to the next section on "Jesus Superior to the Angels" (1:5-2:18) by using τῶν ἀγγέλων again in the first verse of that section. Similarly, at the end of Vaganay's section on "Jesus Superior to the Angels" he refers to Jesus as ἀρχιερεύς (2:17) for the first time. Then at the beginning of the following movement (3:1-5:10) Jesus is called ἀρχιερέα (3:1). This process continues throughout the book, tying each section to the next[30]

Second, Vaganay built on Thien's work, accepting most of his suggested divisions. However, Vaganay understood 1:1-4 to be the introduction of the book, rather than 1:1-2:18, and 1:5-2:18 to set forth the first major theme of Hebrews. He also believed the great central movement on Christ's priesthood to be set forth in three sections, rather than two, and a fifth theme to carry all the way to 13:21, 13:22-25 being the conclusion. When laid out in this manner,

[27] Leon Vaganay, "Le Plan de L'Épître aux Hébreux," in *Memorial Lagrange*, ed. L.-H. Vincent (Paris: J. Gabalda et Cie, 1940), 269-77. Speaking of investigations on the structure of Hebrews, Otto Michel states, "Hier ist zunächst die Untersuchung von L. Vaganay . . . zu nennen, die zwar zunächst wenig Aufsehen erregte, aber doch in der Folgezeit von Wichtigkeit wurde." See Michel, *Der Brief an die Hebräer*, 29.
[28] Vaganay, "Le Plan de L'Épître aux Hébreux," 269.
[29] In ancient Greek rhetoric the practice of tying together sections of material in this fashion was referred to as ὕστερον πρότερον. See Richard Volkmann, *Die Rhetorik der Griechen und Römer in Systematischer Übersicht* (Leipzig: B. G. Teubner, 1885), 438; Michel, *Der Brief an die Hebräer*, 29-31.
[30] Vaganay, "Le Plan de L'Épître aux Hébreux," 271-72.

Introduction (1:1-4)
   I. First Theme in a Single Section: Jesus Superior to the Angels
      (1:5-2:18)

   II. Second Theme in Two Sections: Jesus, Compassionate and
       Faithful High Priest (3:1-5:10)
       A.   First Section: Jesus faithful High Priest (3:1-4:16)
       B.   Second Section: Jesus compassionate High Priest (5:1-10)

   III. Third Theme in Three Sections: Jesus Author of Eternal
        Salvation, Perfect Pontif, Great Priest According to the Order of
        Melchizedek (5:11-10:39)

        Oratorical precautions before embarking on the main subject
        (5:11-6:20)
        A.   First Section: Jesus great priest according to the order of
             Melchizedek (7:1-28)
        B.   Second Section: Jesus perfect pontif (8:1-9:28)
        C.   Third Section: Jesus author of eternal salvation (10:1-39)

   IV. Fourth Theme in Two Sections: Perseverance in the Faith (11:1-
       12:13)
       A.   First Section: Faith (11:1-12:2)
       B.   Second Section: Perseverance (12:3-13)

   V. Fifth Theme in a Single Section: The Great Duty of Holiness
      with Peace (12:14-13:21)

Conclusion:Final Recommendations (13:22-25)

Fig. 4. Vaganay's outline of Hebrews.

the whole book appears to be symmetrical in structure. In Vaganay's outline of Hebrews the first and fifth themes are dealt with in
one section, the second and fourth in two sections, and the third
theme in three sections.

Vaganay's work opened a new era in structural assessments of
Hebrews. Departing from previous approaches, he offered an analysis of the book based on the author's use of rhetorical devices.[31]
Another critic, however, would build upon Vaganay's suggestions
and take center stage in the debate on the structure of Hebrews.[32]

---

[31] So Feld, *Der Hebräerbrief*, 23-25; Vanhoye, *La structure littéraire de l'Épître aux
Hébreux*, 24-25.

[32] In addition to Albert Vanhoye, discussed below, Vaganay also greatly influenced Ceslas Spicq. Spicq's outline of the book is very similar to that of Vaganay. He divided the book, however, into an introduction (1:1-4), four themes (1:5-
2:18, 3:1-5:10, 7:1-10:18, and 10:19-12:29), and an appendix (13:1-19). Notice that
Spicq's fourth theme overlaped both Vaganay's third and fifth themes. Further-

Albert Vanhoye
Albert Vanhoye's monograph, *La structure littéraire de l'Épître aux Hébreux*, endures as the most influential and debated work ever written on the structure of Hebrews. This work, originally published in 1963, with a second edition arriving in 1976, attempted a detailed analysis of the literary devices used in Hebrews.[33] Synthesizing the earlier work of Thien, Gyllenberg, A. Descamps,[34] and especially Vaganay, Vanhoye set forth five "literary devices" the author used to mark the beginnings and endings of sections in the book.[35] These are shown in fig. 5.

The Announcement of the Subject. A sentence or phrase which prepares for the next major section by presenting the theme to be discussed.

Hook Words. A word used *at the end* of one section and *at the beginning* of the next in order to effect a transition between the two and tie the two together.

Change in Genre. Switching back and forth between exposition and exhortation.

Characteristic Terms. Words used a number of times in a section to effect the *physionomie distincte* of that block of material.

Inclusions. The bracketing of a pericope by making a statement at the beginning of the section, an approximation of which is repeated at the conclusion of the section.

Fig. 5. Literary devices in Hebrews, according to Albert Vanhoye.

---

more, Spicq believed the book to develop around four reprises found at 1:1-4, 4:14-16, 8:1-2, and 10:19-22, which he compares in parallel fashion. See Spicq, *L'Épître aux Hébreux*, 33-34.

[33] Vanhoye, *La structure littéraire de l'Épître aux Hébreux*. In the 1976 edition Vanhoye presented fruits of his dialogue with a number of scholars, slightly changing his earlier outline of the book. In addition to his monograph see idem, *Épître aux Hébreux: Texte Grec Structuré* (Rome: Institut Biblique Pontifical, 1967); idem, *Situation du Christ: Hébreux 1-2*, Lectio Divina (Paris: Les Éditions du Cerf, 1969); idem, "Literarische Struktur und theologische Botschaft des Hebräerbriefs (1. Teil)," *Studien für die Neue Testament Umwelt* 4 (1979): 119-47; idem, "Literarische Struktur und theologische Botschaft des Hebräerbriefs (2. Teil)," *Studien für die Neue Testament Umwelt* 5 (1980): 18-49; idem, "Discussions sur la structure de l'Épître aux Hébreux," *Biblica* 52 (1971): 349-80. The last of these articles presents Vanhoye's defense against criticisms raised against his proposals over the previous decade.

[34] A. Descamps, "La structure de l'Épître aux Hébreux," *Revue Diocésaine de Tournai* 9 (1954): 251-58, 333-38.

[35] Vanhoye, *La structure littéraire de l'Épître aux Hébreux*, 37.

The first three devices have already been discussed in considering the works of Rafael Gyllenberg, F. Thien, and Leon Vàganay. "Characteristic terms" refers to the concentrated use of a word or words in a section to establish a primary theme. A. Descamps had, in 1954, published a study of the structure of Hebrews based on this principle and found sections of Hebrews cohering around various terms.[36] For example, "angels" are referred to eleven times in 1:5-2:18, a section Vanhoye called "Le nom bien autre que celui des anges," and only twice thereafter. The term ἄγγελος, therefore, characterizes that block of material. Vanhoye affirmed Descamps findings, suggesting this device must be utilized as one tool among several for assessing Hebrews' structure.[37]

The use of "inclusion," or *inclusio* (the Latin term), is well documented in a variety of ancient literary traditions.[38] *Inclusio* exemplifies a form of distant parallelism and, at times, is related to the chiastic structure of a passage. In an *inclusio* the same components begin and end the unit of text. Variations on a strict *inclusio* include the use of a synonymous or complementary element rather than the same element, and the use of components close to the beginning or end of the unit rather than exactly at the beginning or end.[39] Vanhoye suggested the author of Hebrews used this device to mark the beginnings and endings of each pericope throughout the book.[40]

Highlighting the use of these devices in the text, Vanhoye proposed a symmetrically arranged outline of Hebrews only slightly dissimilar from that of Vaganay.[41] Whereas Vaganay's third section

---

[36] Descamps, "La structure de l'Épître aux Hébreux," 251-58.

[37] Vanhoye, *La structure littéraire de l'Épître aux Hébreux*, 31.

[38] For use of the *inclusio* in ancient Greek literature see Heinrich Lausberg, *Handbuch der literarischen Rhetorik: Eine Grundlegung der Literaturwissenschaft*, 1 (München: Max Hueber, 1960), 317; Volkmann, *Rhetorik der Griechen und Römer in systematischer Übersicht*, 471; Kennedy, George, *Interpretation of the New Testament through Rhetorical Criticism*, (Chapel Hill, NC: The University of North Carolina Press, 1984), 34. For its use in biblical literature see J. Jackson and Martin Kessler, eds., *Rhetorical Criticism: Essays in Honor of James Muilenburg* (Pittsburgh, PA: The Pickwick Press, 1974), 24; Spicq, *L'Épître aux Hébreux*, 31-32. For the use of inclusion in the homiletic pattern discerned by Peder Borgen in John 6 and several works of Philo see Borgen's *Bread From Heaven: An Exegetical Study of the Concept of Manna in the Gospel of John and the Writings of Philo*, Supplements to Novum Testamentum (Leiden: E. J. Brill, 1965), 34-38.

[39] Ivan Jay Ball, *A Rhetorical Study of Zephaniah* (Berkeley, CA: BIBAL Press, 1988), 8.

[40] See Vanhoye, *La structure littéraire de l'Épître aux Hébreux*, 223, 271-303.

[41] Vanhoye put a great deal of emphasis on "*les structures symétriques*" in both the overall discourse and subsections throughout Hebrews. In the monograph Van-

under his third major movement covered 10:1-39, Vanhoye divided
this section into two parts. The first, "cause d'un salut éternel," ran
from 10:1-18 and the second, "Exhortation finale," from 10:19-39,
as demonstrated in fig. 6.[42]

	1,1-4	Introduction	
I	1,5-2,18	The Name Certainly Different than that of the Angels	Doctr.
II A	3,1-4,14	Jesus, Faithful	Paren.
B	4,15-5,10	Jesus, Compassionate High Priest	Doctr.
III p	5,11-6,20	Preliminary Exhortation	Paren.
A	7,1-28	Jesus, High Priest According to the Order of Melchizedek	Doctr.
B	8,1-9,28	Come to Fulfillment	Doctr.
C	10,1-18	Author of Eternal Salvation	Doctr.
f	10,19-39	Final Exhortation	Paren.
IV A	11,1-40	The Faith of the Men of Old	Doctr.
B	12,1-13	The Necessary Endurance	Paren.
V	12,14-13,19	The Peaceful Fruit of Justice	Paren.
	13,20-21	Conclusion	

Fig. 6. Vanhoye's symmetrical outline of Hebrews: "Doctr." = doctrinal;
"Paren." = paraenetic.

Of those offering structural assessments of Hebrews, Vanhoye has
garnered the largest following, some commentators finding in his
use of "literary devices" a convincing, objective means by which the
book must be analyzed.[43] He has also attracted a number of critics

---

hoye dealt with this subject in a separate chapter (pp. 60-63), but would later add
it to his list of literary devices. See *La structure littéraire de l'Épître aux Hébreux*, 60-63;
idem, "Literarische Struktur und theologische Botschaft des Hebräerbriefs (1.
Teil)," 133-41.

[42] Idem, *La structure littéraire de l'Épître aux Hébreux*, 59.

[43] Those who substantially follow Vanhoye are e.g., Attridge, *To the Hebrews*,
16-27; Paul Ellingworth and Eugene Ellingworth, *A Translator's Handbook on the
Letter to the Hebrews* (New York: United Bible Societies, 1983), 341-42; Hugh Montefiore, *A Commentary on the Epistle to the Hebrews*, Black's New Testament Commentaries (London: Adam & Charles Black, 1964), 31; Myles M. Bourke, *The
Epistle to the Hebrews* (Englewood Cliffs, NJ: Prentice Hall, 1990), 922; D. A. Black,

who suggest Vanhoye's proposals have far from satisfied and solved numerous questions on the structure of Hebrews.[44] Despite wideranging criticisms, Vanhoye's detailed analysis demands careful consideration by those taking up structural investigation of the book. One scholar whose proposals have been set over against Vanhoye is Wolfgang Nauck.

The Tripartite Scheme of
Wolfgang Nauck

In an article in the Joachim Jeremias *Festschrift*, Wolfgang Nauck set out to consider the latest proposals on the structure of Hebrews as given by two very influential commentators on the book—Otto Michel and Ceslas Spicq.[45] Michel had offered a tripartite scheme,

---

"The Problem of the Literary Structure of Hebrews," 163-77; and Lane, *Hebrews 1-8*, cii-ciii but see Lane's discussion xc-xcviii. Examples of scholars who have carried out analysis of small sections of Hebrews based on Vanhoye's methodology are Pierre Auffret, "Essai sur la structure littéraire et l'interprétation d'Hébreux 3,1-6," *New Testament Studies* 26 (1980): 380-96; idem, "Note sur la structure littéraire d'Hb ii.1-4," *New Testament Studies* 25 (1979): 166-79; Michel Gourgues, "Remarques sur la 'Structure Centrale' de L'Épitre aux Hébreux," *Revue Biblique* 84 (1977): 26-37.

[44] E.g., James Swetnam, "Form and Content in Hebrews 1-6," *Biblica* 53 (1972): 368-85; idem, "Form and Content in Hebrews 7-13," *Biblica* 55 (1974): 333-48; John Bligh, "The Structure of Hebrews," *The Heythrop Journal* 5 (1964): 175; Philip Edgcumbe Hughes, *A Commentary on the Epistle to the Hebrews* (Grand Rapids, MI: William B. Eerdmans, 1977), 2; T. C. G. Thornton, review of *La structure littéraire de l'Épître aux Hébreux*, by Albert Vanhoye, in *Journal of Theological Studies* 15 (1964): 137-41; Zimmerman, *Das Bekenntnis der Hoffnung*, 20-22. James Swetnam has criticized Vanhoye for at times allowing his literary indicators to overshadow the role of content in the book. He makes the astute observation that

> worthy as this attention to form is, there is a concomitant danger which should not be overlooked: if form is too much divorced from content it can lead to a distortion of content, not a clarification. That is to say, the discovery of form is an arduous undertaking, and if this undertaking is attempted in complete independence of content it can well result in error as to the form. (Swetnam, "Form and Content in Hebrews 1-6," 369)

Vanhoye has interacted with and learned from criticism of his proposals. For example, based on observations by Swetnam, Vanhoye renamed the part "I" of his outline "Situation du Christ" and divided it into two sections: "Intronisation du Fils de Dieu" (1,5-14), an exhortation (2:1-4), and "Solidarité avec les hommes acquise par la Passion glorifiante" (2:5-18). See his response to criticism in "Discussions sur la structure de l'Épître aux Hébreux," 349-80.

[45] Wolfgang Nauck, "Zum Aufbau des Hebräerbriefes," in *Judentum, Urchristentum, Kirche: Festschrift für Joachim Jeremias*, ed. Walther Eltester (Berlin: Alfred Töpelmann, 1960), 199.

dividing the book after 4:13 and 10:18. Spicq, on the other hand, had been greatly influenced by both the methodology and proposals of Leon Vaganay.[46]

While Nauck found Spicq's suggestions *"bestechend,"* he remained unconvinced, primarily on two bases. First, Nauck suggested that the author's use of *Stichworten* is merely a rhetorical device, rather than the *basis* of his arrangement of material. Second, Spicq had built his understanding of the book from the basis of the theological material in Hebrews rather than the hortatory material. Nauck, on the other hand, understood the book to be organized around its paraenetical sections.[47]

Nauck suggested that 1:1-4:13 must be seen as a unit, the sophia-hymn found in 1:2b-3, paralleling the logos-hymn in 4:12-13. The author of Hebrews, according to Nauck, marked his second section (4:14-10:31) with the parallel passages found at 4:14-16 and 10:19-23, as seen in fig. 7.[48]

4:14-16	*10:19-23*
ἔχοντες οὖν ἀρχιερέα μέγαν	ἔχοντες οὖν . . . ἱερέα μέγαν
διεληλυθότα τοὺς οὐρανούς	. . . διὰ τοῦ καταπετάσματος . . .
᾿Ιησοῦν τὸν υἱὸν τοῦ θεοῦ	ἐν τῷ αἵματι ᾿Ιησοῦ
κρατῶμεν τῆς ὁμολογίας	κατέχωμεν τὴν ὁμολογίαν
προσερχώμεθα . . . μετὰ παρρησίας . . .	προσεχώμεθα μετὰ ἀληθινῆς καρδίας . . .

Fig. 7. Wolfgang Nauck's identification of parallels in Heb. 4:14-16 and 10:19-23.

On the basis of these parallels Nauck extended the end of Michel's middle section (at 10:18) to 10:31. According to Nauck, the final section (10:32-13:17) begins and ends with a similar type of exhortation. Thus, Hebrews may be seen as a discourse with three main divisions, each marked at the beginning and end with parallel pas-

---

[46] Spicq, L'Épître aux Hébreux, 33-34.
[47] Nauck, "Zum Aufbau des Hebräerbriefes," 201-203.
[48] Spicq had noticed four parallel passages, or reprises, at 1:1-4, 4:14-16, 8:1-2, and 10:19-22, which he understood to correspond to four movements in the book. See Sqicq, L'Épître aux Hébreux, 33-34.

sages.[49] Nauck's emphasis on these important parallels has won the approval of several scholars less convinced by Albert Vanhoye's scheme.[50]

THE CURRENT STATE OF RESEARCH

In the past two decades scholars have continued to use a wide variety of methodological approaches to the structure of Hebrews and have continued to arrive at diverse conclusions. In addition to the followers of Vanhoye and Nauck, many continue to organize the book around the "Christ is Superior" motif.[51] Chapter 1 demonstrated that this practice has been the most popular among commentators throughout the past seventeen hundred years. Others, with the recent rise of modern rhetorical criticism of the New Testament, have revived interest in Hebrews as a rhetorical discourse crafted in the fashion of classical oratory.[52] Modern linguistic techniques have also been applied to the structure of Hebrews.[53] While rhetorico-critical and linguistic attempts have yet to win a wide following, they must be seriously considered as presenting alternative perspectives on the text.

With the recent flurry of activity surrounding investigations on the structure of Hebrews, nothing close to a concensus can be attained. David Aune, whose work *The New Testament in its Literary Environment* is an important literary-critical offering, has stated flatly, "The structure of Hebrews remains an unsolved problem."[54] J. C. McCullough has suggested "the discussions about the correct

---

[49] Nauck, "Zum Aufbau des Hebräerbriefes," 200-203.

[50] E.g., Michel, *Der Brief an die Hebräer*, 29-35; Zimmermann, *Das Bekenntnis der Hoffnung*, 18-24.

[51] E.g., Hughes, *A Commentary on the Epistle to the Hebrews*, 2.

[52] E.g., Keijo Nissilä, *Das Hohepriestmotiv in Hebräerbrief: Eine exegetische Untersuchung*, Schriften der Finnischen exegetischen Gesellschaft (Helsinki: Oy Liiton Kirjapaino, 1979); Barnabas Lindars, "The Rhetorical Structure of Hebrews," *New Testament Studies* 35 (1989): 382-406; Übelacker, *Der Hebräerbrief als Appell*.

[53] E.g., L. Dussaut, *Synopse Structurelle de l'Épître aux Hébreux: Approache d'Analyse Structurelle* (Paris: Les Éditions du Cerf, 1981); Linda Lloyd Neeley, "A Discourse Analysis of Hebrews," *Occasional Papers in Translation and Textlinguistics* 3-4 (1987): 1-146. Übelacker, mentioned in the previous footnote, also uses linguistics in his study. However, his approach is predominantly in line with rhetorical criticism as espoused by George Kennedy.

[54] David E. Aune, *The New Testament in its Literary Environment*, Library of Early Christianity (Philadelphia, PA: Westminster Press, 1987), 213.

outline and literary structure for the epistle will continue for some time."[55]

While highlighting trends and major turning points in discussions on the structure of Hebrews, the "History of Investigation" has raised a number of questions. Why has the structure of Hebrews remained so elusive? Why do scholars disagree about main turning points in the book? What currently-used methodologies offer concrete insights into the organization of this complex work and which depend more on subjective speculations of the investigator? Indeed, did the author of Hebrews have an organizational principle around which he developed the discourse? Such questions invite an analysis of various outlines and approaches of the modern era.

---

[55] McCullough, "Some Recent Developments in Research on the Epistle to the Hebrews," 156.

CHAPTER TWO

CATEGORIZATION AND EVALUATION OF APPROACHES TO THE STRUCTURE OF HEBREWS

INTRODUCTION

As observed in Chapter 1, a lack of consensus marks the current state of discussions on the structure of Hebrews. Scholars in the past one hundred years have offered schemes with two, three, four, five, six, seven, and even more, primary divisions.[1] Yet even among those who agree on the number of main sections, confusion concerning important dividing points abounds, as demonstrated in fig. 8.[2]

For example, Simon Kistemaker considers the exhortation at 2:1-4 to form a unit with the exposition which follows in 2:5-18. James Swetnam, D. Eduard Riggenbach, and Bernhard Weiss, however, consider 2:1-4 to be the hortatory conclusion to the argument in chapter 1. Albert Vanhoye and Rafael Gyllenberg consider

---

[1] E.g., two-part: Donald Guthrie, *New Testament Introduction* (Downers Grove, IL: Inter-varsity Press, 1976), 728-33. Three-part: D. Eduard Riggenbach, *Der Brief an die Hebräer*, Kommentar zum Neuen Testament (Leipzig: A. Deichert'sche, 1913), 27; Alexander Nairne, *The Epistle of Priesthood: Studies in the Epistle to the Hebrews* (Edinburg: T. & T. Clark, 1913), 302-80; Nauck, "Zum Aufbau des Hebräerbriefes," 203; Zimmermann, *Das Bekenntnis der Hoffnung, 20-21; Michel, Der Brief an die Hebräer*, 8; Franz Joseph Schierse, *Verheißung und Heilsvollendung: Zur theologischen Grundfrage des Hebräerbriefes*, Münchener Theologische Studien (München: Karl Zink Verlag, 1954), 207-209. Four-part: Spicq, *L'Épître aux Hébreux*, 33-35. Five-part: Vaganay, "Le Plan de l'Épître aux Hébreux," 269-77; Vanhoye, "Literarische Struktur und theologische Botschaft des Hebräerbriefs (1. Teil)," 142-43; Gyllenberg, "Die Komposition des Hebräerbriefs," 137-47; Attridge, *The Epistle to the Hebrews*, 17-19; Swetnam, "Form and Content in Hebrews 7-13," 333-43; Simon J. Kistemaker, *Exposition of the Epistle to the Hebrews*, New Testament Commentary (Grand Rapids, MI: Baker Book House, 1984), 18. Six-part: George W. Buchanan, *To the Hebrews*, The Anchor Bible (Garden City, NY: Doubleday & Co.), xxxi; Hughes, *The Epistle to the Hebrews*, 3-4; R. C. H. Lenski, *The Interpretation of the Epistle to the Hebrews and the Epistle of James* (Columbus, OH: The Wartburg Press, 1946), 27. Seven-part: F. F. Bruce, *The Epistle to the Hebrews*, New International Commentary on the New Testament (Grand Rapids, MI: William B. Eerdmans, 1964), lxiii-lxiv.

[2] Cf. the chart by Walter Übelacker in *Der Hebräerbrief als Appell*, 46.

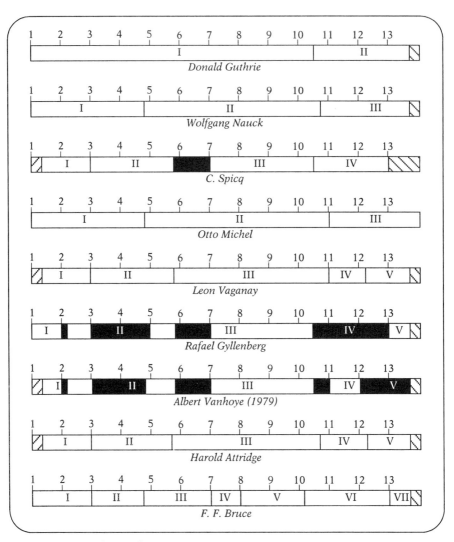

1, 2, 3, etc. = chapter divisions
I, II, III, etc. = primary sections
⬜ = introduction (when emphasized in the outline)
⬜ = conclusion or appendix (when emphasized in the outline)
⬛ = hortatory material (when emphasized as strategic in the outline)

Fig. 8. Approaches to the structural divisions of Hebrews.

the same four verses to be a paraenetic excursus which stands between 1:5-14 and 2:5-18.[3]
The role of 4:14-16 has also been disputed. Wolfgang Nauck, F. F. Bruce, and Franz Joseph Schierse understand the passage to form the introduction to the following section of Hebrews. Alexander Nairne, Gyllenberg, and George Buchanan consider it the conclusion to the section which precedes it. Vaganay, Vanhoye, Spicq, and Harold Attridge, rejecting 4:14-16 as a primary dividing point, all place it in the middle of the book's second movement. These commentators variously understand the section on Christ's highpriesthood to begin at 3:1 (Vaganay, Vanhoye [1979] and Spicq), 4:14 (Nauck and Bruce), 5:1 (Gyllenberg and Buchanan), and 7:1 (Swetnam).[4]
Confusion also surrounds the end of the division on Christ's highpriestly offering. Donald Guthrie, Spicq, Nairne, Bruce, and Lenski break off the section at 10:18. Harold Attridge extends the section to 10:25, Nauck to 10:31, and Michel to 10:39.[5]

APPROACHES TO THE STRUCTURE OF HEBREWS

How have these scholars made decisions concerning where the author of Hebrews ended one section and started the next? These decisions, either consciously or subconsciously, were born of methodology. Such decisions must have been made on the basis of an understanding of how turning points in a discourse are discerned.

---

[3] Kistemaker, *Exposition of the Epistle to the Hebrews*, vi; Swetnam, "Form and Content in Hebrews 7-13," 333; Riggenbach, *Der Brief an die Hebräer*, 27; Weiss, *Kritisch Exegetisches Handbuch über den Brief an die Hebräer*, 34; Vanhoye, "Literarische Struktur und theologische Botschaft des Hebräerbriefs (1. Teil)," 142; Gyllenberg, "Die Komposition des Hebräerbriefs," 137-47.

[4] Nauck, "Zum Aufbau des Hebräerbriefes," 203; Bruce, *The Epistle to the Hebrews*, lxiii; Schierse, *Verheißung und Heilsvollendung*, 207-209; Nairne, *The Epistle of Priesthood*, 302-80; Gyllenberg, "Die Komposition des Hebräerbriefs," 137-47; Buchanan, *To the Hebrews*, xxxi;. Vaganay, "Le Plan de l'Épître aux Hébreux," 269-77; Vanhoye, "Literarische Struktur und theologische Botschaft des Hebräerbriefs (1. Teil)," 142-43; Spicq, *L'Épître aux Hébreux*, 33-35; Attridge, *The Epistle to the Hebrews*, 17-19.

[5] Guthrie, *Introduction to the New Testament*, 728-33; Spicq, *L'Épître aux Hébreux*, 33-35; Nairne, *The Epistle of Priesthood*, 302-80; Bruce, *The Epistle to the Hebrews*, vii-x; Lenski, *The Interpretation of the Epistle to the Hebrews and the Epistle of James*, 27; Attridge, *The Epistle to the Hebrews*, 18-19; Nauck, "Zum Aufbau des Hebräerbriefs," 203; Michel, *Der Brief an die Hebräer*, 8.

At least five distinct approaches to the book's structure have been utilized in recent years. These either offer various suggestions as to the organizational principle around which the book was crafted, or they deny that an organizational principle exists. The approaches may be categorized as "structural agnosticism," "conceptual (or thematic) analysis," "rhetorical criticism," "literary (or rhetorical) analysis," and "linguistic analysis."[6] In the discussion which follows these approaches are assessed for both strengths and weaknesses inherent in each.

Structural Agnosticism

The wide variety of suggestions as to a proper outline for Hebrews illustrates the tremendous complexity of the book. That complexity has led a few scholars to an "agnostic" position on the work's structure similar to Origen's opinion on authorship.[7] At times this agnosticism presents itself passively, the commentator simply failing to attempt any assessment of the book's structure.[8] Others, however, have openly expressed their skepticism concerning the possibility or necessity of discerning a coherent, detailed outline for Hebrews.

James Moffatt, in the Hebrews volume of the *International Critical Commentary*, writes concerning the artificiality of dividing up a discourse like Hebrews, the book, in Moffatt's opinion, not being a theological treatise. He suggests the best course is to follow the argument from point to point.[9] It should be noted that Moffatt is speak-

---

[6] Cf. Vanhoye, *La structure littéraire de l'Épître aux Hébreux*, 13-15; Übelacker, *Der Hebräerbrief als Appell*, 47. Vanhoye divides approaches to the structure of Hebrews into two primary categories: "conceptual" and "literary." Übelacker, on the other hand, provides an overview of approaches which includes the division of theology and warning, the theological angle, temporal divisions, identifying local movement in the book, use of literary criteria, comparison of various sections, and opinions centered in the history of religious ideas.

[7] D. A. Black suggests this comparison saying, "In light of the variety of views on the subject of Hebrews's structure, an open verdict is perhaps a safe course to follow, and here the opinion of Origen on the question of authorship may well be applicable." Black, however, goes on to suggest the unacceptability of this position. He proposes an author of such skill must certainly have illuminated his work. He, therefore, opts for the approach of Albert Vanhoye as the best approach offered thus far in the debate. See Black, "The Problem of the Literary Structure of Hebrews," 175.

[8] E.g., R. M. Wilson, *Hebrews*, New Century Bible Commentary (Grand Rapids, MI: Wm. B. Eerdmans, 1987); Donald A. Hagner, *Hebrews*, New International Biblical Commentary (Peabody, MA: Hendrickson, 1990), 13-14.

[9] James Moffatt, *A Critical Commentary on the Epistle to the Hebrews*, International Critical Commentary (Edinburgh: T. & T. Clark, 1924), xxiii-xxiv.

ing pragmatically concerning the layout of his commentary. He proceeds to divide the book into four main divisions (1:1-4:13; 4:14-7:28; 8:1-10:18; and 10:19-13:25).[10] His statement, however, suggests demarcation of formal divisions and adds nothing to a proper understanding of the text.

Similarly skeptical, T. C. G. Thornton, in his review of the first edition of Albert Vanhoye's monograph, declares the attempt at dividing Hebrews into clearly defined sections may be misguided. He criticizes Vanhoye for forcing later European literary conventions on the author of the book and for not recognizing the author's artistry in making smooth transitions from one topic to another without a significant break in the flow of the discourse.[11]

Thornton's critique falters on at least two points. First, while it is true that the author "did not have to worry about later European literary conventions," there were ancient literary conventions for arranging material in an orderly fashion. Second, when Thornton states, "part of the literary artistry of the writer may well lie in his skill in changing from one topic to another without any appreciable break in the flow of his work," he simply defines the author's use of transitions, a tool utilized extensively in most literary traditions of the world. The use of transitions does not exclude clearly defined turning points in an argument. In fact, the identification of transition techniques may help in placing those turning points.[12]

Perhaps the primary unspoken presupposition behind a "structural agnostic" stance on the outline of Hebrews is that the book's complexity prohibits discernment of an overall, step-by-step development in the author's argument. The question may be put, "How can a discourse which shifts back and forth from genre to genre and topic to topic, repeating previously discussed material, be depicted in a step-by-step structure?" This query seems to be insinuated in both Moffatt and Thornton. Emphasis on the complexity of the work may be seen as a strength of the "agnostic" position. Dynamics in the discourse, such as the author's use of repetition and his change from genre to genre, certainly make analysis of the book's

---

[10] Ibid.

[11] Thornton, review of *La structure littéraire de l'Épître aux Hébreux*, by Albert Vanhoye, 139.

[12] See "Transitions in the Structure of Hebrews" infra, 94-111.

structure an arduous task. The structural agnostic approach to Hebrews, however, stumbles in that it is an argument based on ignorance (i.e., what the commentator has yet to understand). That the
commentator has failed to discern an organizational structure
which he feels adequately portrays development of the author's argument does not necessarily mean no discernible structure exists. In
this sense the approach stands as a passive position rather than an
active methodology.

Conceptual (or Thematic) Analysis

Conceptual analysis refers to assessment of Hebrews' structure
based on discernment of one or more prominent themes around
which the book was organized. This approach normally begins with
a detailed exegesis of the text. Having accomplished the exegesis,
the commentator makes decisions concerning conceptual turning
points in the book and how the various subsections of the discourse
work together toward the author's objective.[13]

As noted above in the "History of Investigation" the most common theme around which an outline of the book has been built is
"Christ is Greater Than . . .," playing off the author's use of
κρείττων. A contemporary example of this approach may be seen in
the work of P. E. Hughes, whose outline of the book is presented in
fig. 9.[14]

---

[13] This approach has been used by most commentators throughout history, e.g.,
all those dealt with in the "History of Investigation" prior to the twentieth century,
with the exceptions of Heinrich Bullinger, Niels Hemmingsen and von Soden. For
other examples see Delitzsch, *Commentary on the Epistle to the Hebrews*, 3; John H. A.
Ebrard, *Biblical Commentary on the Epistle to the Hebrews*, Clark's Foreign Theological
Library, trans. John Fulton (Edinburgh: T. & T. Clark, 1853), v-vii; Lünemann,
Critical and Exegetical Handbook to the Epistle to the Hebrews, 57-62; Riggenbach, *Der
Brief an die Hebräer*, 27; Schierse, *Verheißung und Heilsvollendung*, 207-209; Westcott,
The Epistle to the Hebrews, xlviii-li; Lenski, *Interpretation of the Epistle to the Hebrews*, 27;
Rendall, *The Epistle to the Hebrews*, 1-6; Kistemaker, *Exposition on the Epistle to the
Hebrews*, vi.

[14] One very noticeable problem with this depiction of Hebrews is that Hughes
forces the outline at points. For example, the first main section has been given the
title "Christ Superior to the Prophets" (1:1-3). Yet, is Christ's superiority to the
prophets the main point of that passage? The second section, "Christ is Superior to
Angels," runs, according to Hughes, from 1:4-2:18. Yet, 2:5-18 has to do with
Christ becoming lower than the angels in order to suffer and die. Again, Hughes
has designated 3:1-4:13 "Christ Superior to Moses." However, Moses is discussed
only in 3:2-19 and even there it is questionable whether he is the main topic of
discussion. Thus, blocks of material are forcibly subsumed under a thematic designation which does not adequately reflect the content of that section of material.

I.	Christ Superior to the Prophets	1:1-3
II.	Christ Superior to the Angels	1:4-2:18
III.	Christ Superior to Moses	3:1-4:13
IV.	Christ Superior to Aaron	4:14-10:18
V.	Christ Superior as a New and Living Way	10:19-12:29
VI.	Concluding Exhortations, Requests, and Greetings	13:1-25

Fig. 9. P. E. Hughes' thematically oriented outline of Hebrews.

Franz J. Schierse rejects the "better than" motif as the organizational concept behind the book. Instead he highlights the "promise" theme, outlining the three primary divisions of the book as "The Church and the Word of Promise" (1:1-4:13), "The Church and the Work of Promise (=διαθήκη)" (4:14-10:31), and "The Church and the End of the Promise" (10:32-13:25).[15]

F. F. Bruce offers another alternative, which David Black calls "the patchwork approach."[16] Rather than building an outline around any single concept, he simply divides the book into eight sections, providing each with a title he deems appropriate to the content found in that section. Bruce's sections are "The Finality of Christianity" (1:1-2:18); "The True Home of the People of God" (3:1-4:13); "The High Priesthood of Christ" (4:14-6:20); "The Order of Melchizedek" (7:1-28); "Covenant, Sanctuary, and Sacrifice" (8:1-10:18); "Call to Worship, Faith, and Perseverance" (10:19-12:29); "Concluding Exhortation and Prayer" (13:1-21); and "Postscript" (13:22-25).[17]

The most important presupposition behind the conceptual analysis approach is the adequacy of the investigator's ability to identify topical turns in the discourse. Yet, as clearly demonstrated by the disparity in the outlines of Hebrews, the riddle of the book's structure has not been so easily answered.

The characteristic of Hebrews which proves especially challenging for a conceptual analysis is the use of repetition. The author mentions a topic and then leaves it, only to pick it up at a later point

---

[15] Schierse, *Verheißung und Heilsvollendung*, 207-209.
[16] Black, "The Problem of the Literary Structure of Hebrews," 163.
[17] Bruce, *The Epistle to the Hebrews*, lxiii.

in the argument. For example, Jesus is called "high priest" at 2:17 and 3:1. The designation temporarily falls to the side in the discourse and re-enters at 4:14-5:10. It again is dropped until its appearance at 6:20. Where, then, does the section on "The High Priesthood" begin? An adequate approach to the structure of Hebrews must include a means of assessing use of repetition since the author's argument appears to be more a tapestry than a step-by-step progression of ideas.

Another weakness evidenced in thematically-oriented approaches stems from their propensity toward organization around the expository sections of the book. As Harold Attridge notes, "These construals do little to indicate the function of the various sections of the text and often skew the interpretation of the text as primarily a dogmatic work."[18] To cite but two examples, Hughes' outline in fig. 9 suggests that 1:4-2:18 and 3:1-4:13 have a similar function, each teaching about the superiority of Christ over an Old Testament institution. Yet, 3:1-4:13 is hortatory—there has been a change in genre. Hughes' outline in no way reflects the change in genre or its inherent change in function.

Similarly, Bruce names 3:1-4:13 "The True Home of the People of God." However, the purpose of that passage does not seem to be to teach about the true home expositionally but to exhort the hearers to move on toward that true home. Again, the thematic outline which Bruce presents offers no indication that the author has changed from expository to hortatory discourse.

As Albert Vanhoye suggests the conceptual approach depends on the ability of the commentator to subjectively discern the flow of the author's argument. How then is one to choose between all the subjectively-arrived-at positions? The analyst stands in a quandary since this approach fails to offer objective, structurally-oriented data by which an outline of the book may be agreed upon.[19]

However, the strengths of the thematic approach must not be overlooked. First, it serves to emphasize the commensurate relationship between structure and content. Although the conceptual content of Hebrews proves an inadequate source for determining the structure of that work, a "correct" structural assessment of the book should shed light on the content of the book. Second, blocks of the

[18] Attridge, *The Epistle to the Hebrews*, 14.
[19] Vanhoye, *La structure littéraire de l'Épître aux Hébreux*, 12.

author's material do bond around recognizable themes. If this were not the case, comprehension of any aspect of the argument would be impossible. This coherence may be used as one aspect of a method for analyzing the book's structure.

Rhetorical Criticism

Analysis of New Testament texts in light of ancient Greek literary conventions has a long history.[20] However, the past quarter century has witnessed a fresh interest in such considerations. The current interest in rhetorical studies is most often traced back to a programmatic address entitled "Form Criticism and Beyond" delivered by James Muilenberg.[21] Muilenberg, an Old Testament scholar, was concerned with formal features of composition and stylistic patterns in the Hebrew text. He wanted to move investigation of biblical passages beyond the form-critical focus on the similarities between pericopes of a given genre and to consider the artistic expressions of each author.[22]

Rhetorical criticism of the New Testament, however, has developed as a very different discipline associated with the Greek and Roman rhetorical traditions.[23] The rationale for using these tradi-

---

[20] E.g., Hemmingsen, *Commentaria in omnes Epistolas Apostolorum, Pauli, Petri, Iudae, Ioannis, Iacobi, et in eam quae ad Hebraeos inscribitur*, 831; von Soden, *Der Brief an die Hebräer*, 8-11; Haering, "Gedankengang und Grundgedanken des Hebräerbriefs," 153; Windisch, *Der Hebräerbrief*, 8.

[21] James Muilenberg, "Form Criticism and Beyond," *Journal of Biblical Literature* 88 (1969): 1-18. For detailed histories of the rise of rhetorical criticism as a discipline see Burton L. Mack, *Rhetoric and the New Testament* (Minneapolis, MN: Fortress Press, 1990), 19-24; Duane Frederick Watson, *Invention, Arrangement, and Style: Rhetorical Criticism of Jude and 2 Peter*, Society of Biblical Literature Dissertation Series (Atlanta, GA: Scholars Press, 1988), 1-8.

[22] Muilenberg, "Form Criticism and Beyond," 4-8.

[23] E.g., Kennedy, *New Testament Interpretation through Rhetorical Criticism*; Hans-Dieter Betz, "The Literary Composition and Function of Paul's Letter to the Galatians," *New Testament Studies* 21 (1975): 353-79; idem, *Galatians: A Commentary of Paul's Letter to the Churches in Galatia*, Hermeneia (Philadelphia, PA: Fortress Press, 1979); idem, *2 Corinthians 8 and 9: A Commentary on Two Administrative Letters of the Apostle Paul*, Hermeneia (Philadelphia, PA: Fortress Press, 1985); Robert Jewett, "Romans as an Ambassadorial Letter," *Interpretation* 36 (1982): 5-20; Mack, *Rhetoric and the New Testament*, 31-92; Watson, *Invention, Arrangement, and Style*; Wilhelm Wuellner, "Paul's Rhetoric of Argumentation in Romans," *Catholic Biblical Quarterly* 38 (1976): 330-51; idem, "Where is Rhetorical Criticism Taking Us?," *Catholic Biblical Quarterly* 49 (1987): 448-63.

tions as a means of analyzing the New Testament goes as follows. The books of the New Testament were crafted in the context of Greek culture. At the educational center of that culture stood a highly systematized form of rhetoric, extensively documented in the educational handbooks of that era. Even those writers of the New Testament who had no formal training would have been exposed to and influenced by public speeches.[24] Thus, patterns of rhetorical argumentation as explained in the Greco-Roman handbooks can be identified in the New Testament.

Rhetorical criticism of the New Testament, taking its cue from the "New Rhetoric" of Chaim Perelman and L. Olbrechts-Tyteca, also places a great deal of emphasis on argument as an aspect of rhetorical literature.[25] This constitutes another step away from (or beyond) Muilenberg's stylistically-oriented approach. While still giving attention to features of style, New Testament rhetorical critics seek to understand the dynamic of persuasion and its function in social contexts.[26]

The older works of Niels Hemmingsen, Hermann F. von Soden, Theodore Haering, and Hans Windisch already mentioned perceive the book of Hebrews as structured according to patterns in ancient Greek oratory.[27] These works, of course, antedated the recent rise of modern rhetorical criticism of the New Testament. Yet they do share a common interest in insights gained by analyzing New Testament works in light of a Hellenistic rhetorical context.

---

[24] E.g., Burton Mack points out that in Palestine alone there were over thirty Hellenistic cities during the time of Jesus, twelve within a twenty-five mile radius of Nazareth. These Greek cities would have had schools, theaters, and active markets where speeches would have been given constantly. See Mack, *Rhetoric and the New Testament*, 29.

[25] Mack, *Rhetoric and the New Testament*, 19-21; Wuellner, "Where is Rhetorical Criticism Taking Us?;" 449; Chaim Perelmann and L. Olbrechts-Tyteca, *The New Rhetoric: A Treatise on Argumentation*, trans. John Wilkinson and Purcell Weaver (Notre Dame: Notre Dame University Press, 1969).

[26] Perhaps the most systematic approach to rhetorical criticism of the New Testament presented thus far may be found in George Kennedy's *New Testament Interpretation through Rhetorical Criticism*. Kennedy outlines five steps in his approach: (1) determine the rhetorical unit; (2) analyze the rhetorical situation; (3) determine the species of rhetoric (i.e., judicial, deliberative, or epideictic), the question, and the stasis; (4) analyze invention, arrangement, and style; and (5) evaluate rhetorical effectiveness. See Kennedy, *New Testament Interpretation through Rhetorical Criticism*, 33-38.

[27] Supra, 5-8.

Several recent attempts have been made to analyze the book through rhetorico-critical methodology. For example, Barnabas Lindars seeks to review the whole book from the standpoint of the rhetorical effect upon the readers and suggests Hebrews falls in the category of deliberative rhetoric with its advising and dissuading.[28] His analysis, however, offers little help on structural considerations of the work; he merely comments on the possible impact of each section on the hearers.

A much more extensive and astute contribution has been made by Walter G. Übelacker in *Der Hebräerbrief als Appell: Untersuchungen zu exordium, narratio und postscriptum.* Übelacker believes Hebrews to be a deliberative discourse with a *prooemium,* i.e., exordium (1:1-4), *narratio* with *propositio* (1:5-2:18), *argumentatio* with *probatio* and *refutatio* (3:1-12:29), *peroratio* (13:1-21), and *postscriptum* (13:22-25). His work on 1:1-4 presents perhaps the most extensive analysis available on that passage.[29] Übelacker primarily deals with the exordium and to a lesser extent with 1:5-2:18 which he labels the *narratio.* His suggestions as to the nature of the rest of the book flow from the analysis of these passages.

Another interesting study has been set forth by Keijo Nissilä in *Das Hohepriestermotiv im Hebräerbrief: Eine exegetische Untersuchung.* Nissilä aims to analyze the function of the high priest motif in the development of the author's discussion.[30] He examines nine passages in Hebrews—2:14-18, 3:1-6, 4:14-16, 5:1-10, 7:26-28, 8:1-6, 9:11-15, 9:24-28, and 10:11-14—running each through a *Textanalyse,* involving consideration of structure, style, context, and the range of ideas, followed by *Motivanalyse.* The latter begins with the "problem," or questions raised by the passage. Then Nissilä analyzes the author's use of the high priest motif as it relates to other prominent motifs in the book. The *Motivanalyse* of each pericope ends with consideration of *die rhetorische Anwendung,* or rhetorical use of the high priest motif in that passage.[31] Nissilä concludes that the high priest motif serves functionally as a rhetorical element used by the author to teach, admonish, delight, and reprove his listeners. He

[28] Lindars, "The Rhetorical Structure of Hebrews," 382-406.
[29] Übelacker, *Der Hebräerbrief als Appell,* 66-138.
[30] Nissilä, *Das Hohepriestermotiv im Hebräerbrief,* 1-5.
[31] Ibid., 15-19. The author concludes the book with a consideration of the motif in the hortatory material found after 10:18 (pp. 245-76).

also suggests the motif stands as the key *structural* element binding
the whole discourse together. Nissilä's outline of the book has similarities with other rhetorical analyses, dividing the work into *exordium* (1:1-4), *narratio* (1:5-2:18), *argumentatio* (3:1-12:29), and *epilogus*
(13:1-25).[32]

The studies contributed by Übelacker and Nissilä both utilize
insights from ancient rhetorical practice to assess the argument of
Hebrews. Both also use aspects of modern text linguistics, sometimes
referred to as "discourse analysis" in the United States, to examine
textual dynamics in the book. In addition, each of these authors
makes an assessment of the structure of the whole book based on
analysis of parts of the book.

While the works of Übelacker and Nissilä offer numerous insights
into some aspects of Hebrews, the wholesale approach of pegging
Hebrews as a Greek oration in the style of the rhetorical schools
presents several difficulties. First, Hebrews is not easily categorized
according to any one speech form of ancient Greek rhetoric.[33] It not
only involves elements which are in line with deliberative speeches,
meant to persuade or dissuade, but also contains elements of epideictic, which consisted of public praise or blame of a given person.
The general pattern used by Übelacker is primarily applicable to
forensic rhetoric.

Second, while the speech forms in the classical handbooks were
crafted in the judicial and political spheres, the book of Hebrews has
the characteristics of the hellenistic synagogue homily. This form,
while containing a wide range of rhetorical features described in the
Greek handbooks, can not be forced into the mold of a classical
speech. Rather, the author's means of argument follow the rhetoric
and exegetical skills of the rabbis.[34]

---

[32] Ibid., 74-78, 143-47, 239-44.

[33] The rhetorical critics admit that most of the Christian literature is difficult to
categorize. Burton Mack states, "Early Christian rhetoric was a distinctively
mixed bag in which every form of rhetorical issue and strategy was frequently
brought to bear simultaneously in an essentially extravagant persuasion" (*Rhetoric
and the New Testament*, 35). Duane Watson classifies Jude as deliberative rhetoric
but then admits "this classification is too neat, for the bulk of Jude (vv. 4-19) is
clearly of a demonstrative nature . . ." Due to the "epideictic" overtones of the
book he clarifies his classification as "deliberative rhetoric which relies heavily
upon epideictic" (Watson, *Invention, Arrangement, and Style*, 32-33).

[34] See especially Thyen, *Der Stil des jüdisch-hellenistischen Homilie*, 16-17. For other
works on Hebrews as a sermon see Grässer, "Der Hebräerbrief 1938-1963," 159-

Third, the assigning of general designations (e.g., *exordium*, *narratio*, *argumentatio*, etc.) to large sections of the book is not particularly illuminative of the literary dynamics and structure of the text.[35] Even if such designations could be argued conclusively, they speak more of function of general blocks of material.

These weaknesses should overshadow neither the helpful emphases of rhetorical criticism nor the specific insights of Übelacker and Nissilä. Patterns of style in Hebrews do correspond to Greek conventions and the author has long been recognized as a practiced scholar in his use of the Greek language. Therefore, comparisons as to style can be made. Also, rhetorical criticism's recent emphasis on patterns of argumentation is instructive. Units within the broader discourse of Hebrews may be isolated and the elements of those units analyzed as to their "persuasive functions" within that unit.

Literary (or Rhetorical) Analysis

Works on the structure of Hebrews such as those by Leon Vaganay, Albert Vanhoye, Ceslas Spicq, Wolfgang Nauck, Rafael Gyllenberg, and James Swetnam may be classified in differing degrees as "literary," or "rhetorical" analyses. The designation "literary analysis" refers to an examination of the text which focuses on literary characteristics by which the author crafted his work. These include characteristics which mark the structure (e.g., *inclusio*, chiasmus, etc.), aspects of style, use of diverse genres, repetition, and vocabulary. This type of analysis may also be referred to as "rhetorical" as that term is used by James Muilenberg, a pioneer of modern rhetorical criticism.[36]

As noted in the "History of Investigation," the proposals of Vanhoye and Nauck have received the greatest attention. In a pair of articles published in 1979 and 1980, Vanhoye updated his views concerning the structure of Hebrews. These articles, in conjunction

---

60; Lane, "Hebrews: A Sermon in Search of a Setting," 13-18; James Swetnam, "On the Literary Genre of the 'Epistle' to the Hebrews," *Novum Testamentum* 11 (1969): 261-68.

[35] So Attridge, *To the Hebrews*, 16.

[36] Muilenberg, "Form Criticism and Beyond," 1-3. This use of the word "rhetorical" refers much more to *style* than to argument. The author's building of an argument is a primary emphasis of the rhetorical criticism being used in New Testament circles (supra, 29-30).

with the second edition of Vanhoye's monograph, embody the best
of proposals set forth by Vaganay, Gyllenberg, Swetnam, and
Spicq.[37] Vanhoye uses "announcement of a theme," "hook words,"
"change in genre," "characteristic words," "inclusion," and "symmetrical alignment" (i.e., chiasmus) as literary indicators of structure in the book.[38]

Several strengths emerge in Vanhoye's methodology. First, hook
words, inclusions, and chiasmus were all used as literary devices in
the ancient world. Vanhoye's approach takes seriously the historical and literary contexts in which the book of Hebrews was produced. This does not, of course, mean that Vanhoye has accurately
detected the use of such devices in Hebrews. However, such devices
must be considered as viable tools which an author of the time had
at his disposal.

Second, Vanhoye highlights the switch back and forth between
exposition and exhortation in Hebrews. A change in genre may
mark a shift in the author's discourse. Since the author of Hebrews
uses this device as a prominent tool in the development of the book,
it must be considered as one possible factor in the book's structure.

Third, Vanhoye detects "announcement of a theme" consistently
throughout the book of Hebrews. The fact that scholars such as
J. A. Bengel, F. Thien, Leon Vaganay, and Vanhoye have, in varying degrees, noticed its use carries weight. Any investigation into
the book's structure must consider this phenomenon.

Finally, the use of "characteristic words" may be affirmed as one
device used by authors in building semantic cohesion in various
sections of a discourse. Since an author builds and develops his
message partially on the basis of lexical choices, the use of vocabulary must be considered as one possible factor through which a shift
in the discourse might be demonstrated.

The highlighting of such literary devices does provide objective
means for determining the beginning and ending points in sections
of the book—if the use of such devices can be conclusively demonstrated. Furthermore, the "literary" method does not necessarily

---

[37] Vanhoye, *La structure littéraire de l'Épître aux Hébreux*; idem, "Literarische Struktur und theologische Botschaft des Hebräerbrief (1. Teil)," 119-47; idem, "Literarische Struktur und theologische Botschaft des Hebräerbrief (2. Teil)," 18-49.

[38] In his monograph Vanhoye lists the first five and then deals with the sixth in a
separate chapter. See *La structure littéraire de l'Épître aux Hébreux*, 60-63.

conflict with use of conceptual analysis or rhetorical criticism; rather, these methods have complementary concerns.

For example, identification of "characteristic terms" in literary analysis touches upon the thematic interest of conceptual analysis. With rhetorical criticism literary analysis shares an interest in matters of style and the *milieu* in which the book was originally written. The literary approach, moreover, avoids the subjectivity of conceptual analysis and the rhetorico-critical pitfall of forcing a work into the pattern of a particular Greco-Roman oratory form.

However, literary analysis as used by Vanhoye has its own shortcomings. The use of "characteristic words" presents merely one approach by which the semantic cohesion of a block of material may be demonstrated. Suggestions made in modern linguistic studies concerning cohesion of pericopes might be used to strengthen analysis of semantic cohesion in Hebrews. Vanhoye also has been criticized for forcing his identification of literary devices at points and giving "form" priority over "content" in his structural assessment of the book.[39]

In the ongoing debate over the structure of Hebrews, Vanhoye has failed to answer adequately Wolfgang Nauck's highlighting of the parallels found at 4:14-16 and 10:19-23, dismissing them as insignificant.[40] It may be argued that these two passages contain the most prominent use of parallelism in the whole book. Since such parallels normally are used by Vanhoye to mark inclusions, and since he does not give an adequate account of the parallels in these passages, he might be accused of being inconsistent in his methodology at this point.

Linguistic Analysis

A fifth general approach to analyzing the structure of Hebrews concerns use of linguistics. Linguistics may be defined simply as "the study of human language" and is especially concerned with the "inner workings" of language, or the various aspects of a language which must work together to accomplish an act of communication (e.g., speech sounds, word meanings, grammar, word group-

---

[39] Swetnam, "Form and Content in Hebrews 1-6," 369.
[40] Nauck, "Zum Aufbau des Hebräerbriefes," 200-203; Vanhoye, "Discussions sur la structure de l'Épître aux Hébreux," 365.

ing in phrases, sentences, paragraphs, etc.).[41] Since publication of
James Barr's vastly influential work, *The Semantics of Biblical Lan-*
guage, a plethora of published materials have been offered applying
various aspects of linguistics to biblical literature.[42] At least two
such works have presented full-scale analyses of the book of Hebrews.

First, in 1981 Louis Dussaut published *Synopse Structurelle de L'É-*
pître aux Hébreux: Approche d'Analyse Structurelle. Dussaut described his
work as based on the new tagmemics, which he defined as concerned with "l'ordre des mots et de leurs unités rédactionnelles dans
la totalité du texte . . ."[43] Dussaut's aim was to present a synopsis of
the book based on an "analyse structurelle" involving an index
system by which he tracked vocables throughout the book. These
vocables were analyzed in a given section and then in the book as a
whole. Each section was shown to be unified both structurally and
conceptually. Then the sections were set forth as symmetrically related to each other. He concluded Hebrews has fourteen major
sections laid out in three parts (1:1-5:10; 5:11-10:39; 11:1-13:21/25).
The first part has two columns of material, the second three, and
the third two.[44]

A second linguistic method utilized in examination of Hebrews is
the "discourse analysis" (i.e., "text linguistics") of Linda L. Neeley.[45] Discourse analysis is an approach to examining a text by

---

[41] Black, *Linguistics for Students of New Testament Greek*, 4-5.

[42] For overviews see Anthony C. Thiselton, "Semantics and New Testament
Interpretation," in *New Testament Interpretation: Essays on Principles and Methods*, ed.
I. Howard Marshall (Grand Rapids, MI: Wm. B. Eerdmans, 1977), 75-104; David
Allen Black, *Linguistics, Biblical Semantics, and Bible Translation: An Annotated Bibliog-*
raphy of Periodical Literature from 1961 (La Mirada, CA: Biola University, 1984);
Moisés Silva, *Biblical Words and Their Meanings: An Introduction to Lexical Semantics*
(Grand Rapids, MI: Zondervan Publishing House, 1983), 17-22.

[43] Dussaut, *Synopse Structurelle de L'Épître aux Hébreux*, 5.

[44] Ibid., 5-18. Dussaut has been greatly influenced by the conclusions of Albert
Vanhoye (see Ibid., 3-4). His break-down of the book into sections follows Vanhoye closely. While Dussaut offers interesting thoughts on the means by which
unity of a section may be demonstrated, it is at least possible that his foundational
understanding of transition points in the book is derived from Vanhoye, rather
than his own method. In any case, his analysis offers no great advance over Vanhoye's own use of "characteristic terms" and "symmetric structure" in the book.

[45] Neeley, "A Discourse Analysis of Hebrews," 1-146. The "discourse analysis"
method is more commonly referred to as "text linguistics" outside North America.
See Klaus Berger, *Exegese des Neuen Testaments: Neue Wege vom Text zur Auslegung*, 2d
ed. (Heidelberg: Quelle & Meyer, 1984), 11-32.

which the critic seeks to understand the relationships between the various sections of an author's discourse. At the heart of discourse analysis is the endeavor to understand the paragraphs in the discourse. To grasp the semantic content of a whole discourse one can not merely add up the semantic content of each sentence, since sentences themselves are grouped together by an author to form larger units of material (e.g., paragraphs) which have various semantic functions in the development of the discourse.[46]

Neeley follows the discourse analysis method developed by Robert E. Longacre.[47] Longacre lists four major systems of organization which may be used by an author developing a discourse:

> (1) the combining of sentences into larger discourse units—paragraphs, and embedded discourses,[48] (2) functions of discourse units, i.e., constituent structure, (3) distinction between backbone and support information, and (4) semantic organization.[49]

Neeley analyzes Hebrews on the basis of each of these systems of information organization.

Her first chapter, "Determining Discourse Units," examines how the discourse units in Hebrews may be isolated. Neeley proposes there are four major criteria which should be used in determining discourse divisions. These are (1) a change in genre; (2) transition introductions or conclusions; (3) use of relatively rare linguistic devices; and (4) evidence of the unity of the preceding embedded discourse (its lexical and semantic cohesion).[50]

---

[46] J.P. Louw, *The Semantics of New Testament Greek*, The Society of Biblical Literature Semeia Studies (Philadelphia, PA: Fortress Press, 1982), 97-98.

[47] Neeley, "A Discourse Analysis of Hebrews," 1. See Robert E. Longacre, "Some Fundamental Insights of Tagmemics," *Language* 41 (1965): 66-76; idem, *The Grammar of Discourse*, Topics in Language and Linguistics (New York: Plenum Press, 1983); idem, *An Anatomy of Speech Notions* (Lisse, Belgium: Peter de Ridder Press, 1976); idem, *Tagmemics* (Waco, TX: Word, 1985).

Longacre, who teaches at the University of Texas at Arlington and is associated with the Summer Institute of Linguistics in Dallas, TX, has done extensive work with the Wycliff Bible Translators, a group dedicated to translating the Bible into numerous modern languages.

[48] I.e., smaller discourses within a main discourse.

[49] Neeley, "A Discourse Analysis of Hebrews," 1.

[50] Ibid., 6. The first three of these criteria roughly parallel Vanhoye's analysis of literary devices. The "change in genre" matches Vanhoye's "third criterion;" "transition introductions and conclusions" correspond to Vanhoye's "announcement of a subject" but also relate to his "inclusions" and "hook words," devices which could also be placed under Neeley's "relatively rare linguistic devices."

"Change in genre" refers, once again, to the author's shift back
and forth between exposition and exhortation.[51] Back-references (of
which one category is "hook words"), reiterations, and summaries
are subsumed under "transition introductions or conclusions." Under her examination of linguistic devices she mentions the use of
rhetorical questions, rare particles, and the use of vocatives. Neeley
also refers to an *inclusio* (without calling it such) at 5:10b and 6:20.
She later deals with inclusions (referred to as "sandwich structures") under her discussion on "lexical and semantic cohesion."
Other means for determining the semantic unity of a discourse unit
are the recognition of chiasmus and the tracking of characteristic
words.[52]

The second chapter of the article discusses the functions of various constituents (i.e., units with a certain function) which make
up a discourse. For example, Neeley suggests that most well developed discourses (and embedded discourses) have an *introduction*,
various *points* which develop the author's argument, a *peak* (or "climax"), and a *conclusion*.[53] The identification of such constituents in a
discourse can help confirm the structure of the discourse. Based on
these criteria, Neeley isolates the discourse divisions in Hebrews and
sets forth an outline of the book as depicted in fig. 10.[53]

Neeley's outline portrays an overall *constituent structure* of the book.
The constituents are a *thematic introduction* (1:1-4), *point 1* (ED1, 1:1-
4:13), *point 2* (ED2, 4:14-10:18), *peak* (ED3, 10:19-13:21), *conclusion*
(13:20-21), and *finis* (13:22-25).[54] The book consists of three major

---

[51] In modern linguistic theory great emphasis is placed on identification of discourse types as a starting point for analysis. Longacre identifies four primary types:
narrative, procedural, behavioral (i.e., hortatory), and expository. He remarks,
"Characteristics of individual discourses can be neither described, predicted, nor
analyzed without resort to a classification of discourse types. It is pointless to look
in a discourse for a feature which is not characteristic of the type to which that
discourse belongs. See Robert E. Longacre, *The Grammar of Discourse*, 1. Also on the
need to distinguish between types of discourse see Joseph E. Grimes, *The Thread of
Discourse* (Paris: Mouton, 1975), 33.

[52] Neeley, "A Discourse Analysis of Hebrews," 6-18.

[53] Ibid., 3. However, Neeley points out that "A particular discourse or embedded discourse is not required to have all four types of constituents in order to be a
well formed discourse."

[53] Nowhere does Neeley lay out her outline in the following fashion. She shows
her discourse and embedded discourse divisions on pp. 22 and 141 but does not
display these along with their respective themes. The following outline, therefore, is
extracted from her discussions of the discourse units.

[54] Ibid., 41.

discourses (points 1 and 2, and the peak) bracketed on each end by an introduction and a conclusion. A formalized closing, unrelated to the thematic development of the book, occurs at the end.

1:1-4 Thematic Introduction to the Book
Embedded Discourse 1 (1:1-4:13): God Has Spoken to Us in His Son
    Introduction (1:1-4)
    ED 1a (1:1-2:18) The Divinity and Humanity of Christ
    ED 1b (3:1-4:13) Do Not Harden Your Hearts
Embedded Discourse 2 (4:14-10:18): [The Son] as Our High Priest Has
    Offered a Complete Sacrifice for Sins and by this
    Obtained Salvation for Us.
    ED 2a (4:14-6:20) Introduction
    ED 2b (7:1-28) Christ a Superior Priest
    ED 2c (8:1-10:18) Christ's Superior Ministry
Embedded Discourse 3 (10:19-13:21) Therefore Let Us Draw Near to God
    with a True Heart in Full Assurance of Faith . . . Let
    us Hold Fast Our Confession . . . and Let Us Consid-
    er Each Other to Stir Up to Love and Good Works.
    ED 3a (10:19-39) Introduction
    ED 3b (11:1-40) By Faith Endure
    ED 3c (12:1-29) Run the Race
    ED 3d (13:1-21) Practical Exhortation
13:20-21 Conclusion
13:22-25 Finis (Formalized Closing)

Fig. 10. Linda Neeley's discourse analysis assessment of the structure of Hebrews: ED = embedded discourse.

The strength of discourse analysis lies in its attempt to analyze a text as an act of coherent communication built on the basis of identifiable principles of communication found in languages throughout the world. It takes into consideration the use of literary devices, the author's use of various genres, semantic cohesion of individual sections, the roles of subsections of material (i.e., "constituents"), and the overall development of the discourse. This discourse analysis method incorporates strengths found in other methodologies, such as literary analysis, rhetorical criticism, and conceptual analysis.

However, one strength of both literary analysis and rhetorical criticism, which stands as a potential weakness of the linguistic approach, is emphasis on the historical context in which a work was developed. Literary analysis, as practiced by the Vaganay-Vanhoye school, and rhetorical criticism each carry a stress on understanding ancient literary or oratory conventions. The principles

used by Linda Neeley, derived from the method of Robert Longacre, were honed in the study of a wide variety of modern languages. The discourse analysis method could be strengthened by added
study of the ancient context in which a work was developed.

For example, Neeley understands Heb. 11:1-40 to be expository.[55] Michael R. Cosby has demonstrated, however, that the use of
lists of *exempla* was a hortatory device used extensively in the ancient
world to persuade the reader to take some action.[56] While the form
of Heb. 11:1-40 seems to be expository (based on verb tense, the use
of third person nouns and pronouns, etc.)[57], the "surface structure"
at this point is misleading. Neeley thus misunderstands the import
of the passage due to a lack of understanding the historical context.

SUMMARY AND CONCLUSION

Thus far the study has considered past proposals on the structure of
Hebrews and the approaches which led to those proposals. The
History of Investigation in Chapter 1 and the introductory section
of Chapter 2 have served to highlight the great variety of, and
disparity between, suggestions on the book's structure. These suggestions conflict over primary dividing points in the book, the organizational principle around which the author built his work, and
the methodology by which the structure of the book may be discerned.

Five approaches to the structure of Hebrews have been discussed
in the present chapter. The first of these, "structural agnosticism,"
has nothing to offer methodologically. Each of the other four approaches, however, has strengths which should be considered in
formulation of a methodology for a structural examination of Hebrews.

An emphasis on the relationship between structure and content
and the recognition of unifying themes in Hebrews are helpful aspects of conceptual analysis. Rhetorical criticism provides a sensitivity to patterns of both style and argumentation. Literary analysis, as practiced by Albert Vanhoye, heightens the analyst's

---

[55] Ibid., 8.
[56] Michael R. Cosby, "The Rhetorical Composition of Hebrews 11," *Journal of Biblical Literature* 107 (1988): 268.
[57] Neeley, "A Discourse Analysis of Hebrews," 6.

awareness of devices such as "hook words," inclusions, and chiasmus—patterns commonly found in the literature of the New Testament world. Literary analysis also suggests consideration of the author's shift back and forth between the two prominent genres in the book, a concern shared in linguistic investigations. Vanhoye's "characteristic terms" overlaps with identification of lexically cohesive items in a discourse, another aspect of linguistic investigation. Other strengths of the linguistic method include means for identification of unit boundaries and understanding constituent relationships between discourse units.

Chapter 3 attempts to draw upon these various strengths for the formulation of an effective methodology.

PART II

TEXT-LINGUISTIC ANALYSIS OF
THE STRUCTURE OF HEBREWS

CHAPTER THREE

METHOD OF ANALYSIS

INTRODUCTION

At least five distinct approaches have been utilized for investigations into the structure of Hebrews. Properly understood, text linguistics, sometimes referred to as discourse analysis, includes the concerns inherent in three of the other approaches. Analysis of patterns of argumentation, found in rhetorical criticism, may be subsumed under "constituent analysis" in text linguistics. Analysis of elements of style is also a concern of both rhetorical criticism and text linguistics. The sensitivity to thematic development in conceptual analysis and all aspects of literary analysis, as practiced by Albert Vanhoye, also may be subsumed under text linguistics.

However, text-linguistic analysis of Hebrews must include attention to literary and oratorical conventions of the first century.[1] Insights into that *milieu* in which Hebrews was crafted are essential for proper assessment of the book's structure. The methodology presented below, although highly eclectic, may be designated as "text-

---

[1] The author of Hebrews especially uses methods of interpretation and argumentation found in the rabbis. His use of the Old Testament has been one of the most neglected topics in discussions on the structure of the book. For general introductions to the author's use of the Old Testament see Markus Barth, "The Old Testament in Hebrews," in *Issues in New Testament Interpretation*, ed. W. Klassen and G.F. Snyder (New York: Harper and Row, 1962), 65-78; Richard Longenecker, *Biblical Exegesis in the Apostolic Period* (Grand Rapids, MI: William B. Eerdmans, 1975), 158-85; Simon Kistemaker, *The Psalm Citations in the Epistle to the Hebrews* (Amsterdam: Soest, 1961); Caird, "The Exegetical Method of the Epistle to the Hebrews," 44-51; R.E. Clements, "The Use of the Old Testament in Hebrews," *Southwestern Journal of Theology* 28 (1985): 36-45; H. J. B. Combrink, "Some Thoughts on the OT Citations in the Epistle to the Hebrews," *Neotestamentica* 5 (1971): 22-36; Howard George, "Hebrews and OT Quotations," *Novum Testamentum* 10 (1968): 208-16; P. Katz, "The Quotations from Deuteronomy in Hebrews," *Zeitschrift für die neuetestamentliche Wissenschaft* 49 (1958): 213-23; J.C. McCullough, "The Old Testament Quotations in Hebrews," *New Testament Studies* 26 (1979-80): 363-79; K.J. Thomas, "The Old Testament Citations in Hebrews," *New Testament Studies* 11 (1965): 303- 25; J. Van der Ploeg, "L'exégèse de l'Ancien Testament dans l'Épître aux Hébreux," *Revue Biblique* 54 (1947): 187-228.

linguistic analysis." This, however, is a form of text linguistics which seeks to be cognizant of the world and ways in which the author of Hebrews developed and delivered his message.

Text Linguistics

As noted in the discussion of Linda Neeley's examination of Hebrews, text linguistics is an approach to studying a text by which the critic seeks to understand the relationships between sections of an author's discourse.[2] The use of text linguistics in biblical studies is in its infancy. Peter Cotterell and Max Turner note, "The fact is that at the present there are no firm conclusions, no generally accepted formulae, no fixed methodology, not even an agreed terminology."[3] This young discipline, however, offers perspectives and means of analysis which prove helpful in the process of exegesis and examination of structure.

Text-linguistic theory is based on an assumption that written texts begin with the author's conception of the theme which he wants to communicate. This theme is then expressed and developed by the author's language choices—individual words, grammar, and style—which give meaning and structure to the "cola" which make up his "paragraphs."[4] To understand the author's development of

---

[2] In the present study "discourse" refers to a semantic unit of communication which is more than one sentence in length and forms a unified whole. The use of "discourse" here is synonymous with the term "text" as used in some linguistic circles. See M.A.K. Halliday and Ruqaiya Hasan, *Cohesion in English* (London: Longman, 1976), 1. When referring to the *whole* of Hebrews, the designation "main discourse," or "macro-discourse," or simply "discourse," will be used. When referring to smaller units of discourse within the main discourse, the term "embedded discourse" will be used. An embedded discourse may consist of one, or more, paragraph units. "Discourse unit" may refer either to an embedded discourse or one of the paragraphs which make up the embedded discourse.

[3] Peter Cotterell and Max Turner, *Linguistics and Biblical Interpretation* (Downers Grove, IL: InterVarsity Press, 1989), 233.

[4] The term "colon" as used here does not refer to a poetical unit (synonymous with a "stich"), nor divisions of a line of a Greek manuscript. Commenting on the linguistic use of the term, D.A. Black defines a colon as

a unit of grammatical structure with clearly marked external dependencies. It always has either overtly or covertly a central matrix consisting of a nominal element (subject) and a verbal element (predicate), each having the possibility of extended features. Those features which are added to either the nominal or verbal element restrict the range of reference even as they supply further information.

his theme, one must first examine each colon on the lexical, syntactic, and rhetorical levels, as depicted in fig. 11.[5]

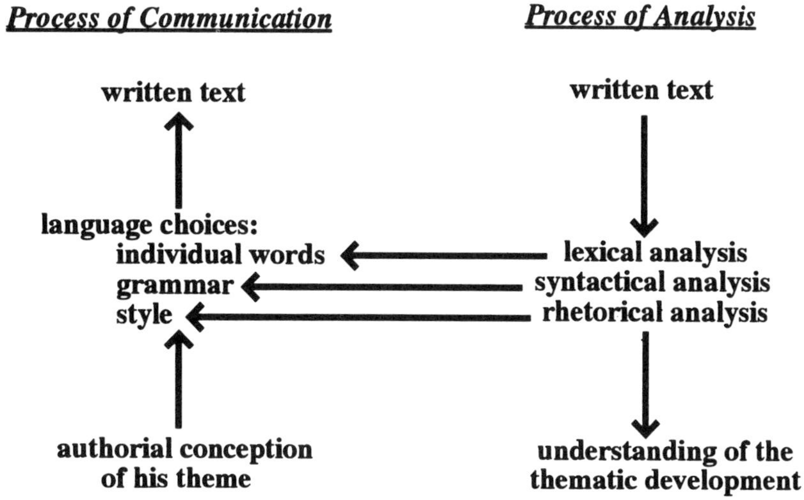

Process of Communication   Process of Analysis

Fig. 11. The processes of communication and analysis.

The goal of lexical, syntactical, and rhetorical analysis of individual cola is, however, to understand the paragraphs which make up the discourse, for it is the paragraph, rather than the colon, which represents the basis for understanding the meaning of the author's main discourse.[6] To understand the semantic content of a whole

---

See D.A. Black, "Hebrews 1:1-4: A Study in Discourse Analysis," *Westminster Theological Journal* 49 (1987): 176-77. This means that a compound sentence may be made up of several cola. In analyzing each colon separately, the researcher is able to focus on the author's propositions which are central to his argument. This method was developed by J.P. Louw in *The Semantics of New Testament Greek* (Philadelphia: Fortress Press, 1982), 67-158.

In the present study the term "paragraph" is used to refer to a tightly knit cluster of cola, which sets forth a unified point used in advancing the discourse. On the hierarchy of units of meaning in a discourse see ibid., 98-99; Cotterell and Turner, *Linguistics and Biblical Interpretation*, 193-94.

[5] Cf. the diagram by J.P. Louw, *The Semantics of New Testament Greek*, 94. The diagram of fig. 11 has developed from discussions with my colleague J. Scott Duvall. The present study does not use the designation "deep structure" but rather "thematic structure." The reason for this is that the former designation has been used at times by the proponents of *structuralism* to refer to processes in the author's subconscious. Our assumption is that the author was conscious of the development of his theme.

[6] Berger, *Exegese des Neuen Testaments*, 11; Black, *Linguistics for Students of New Testament Greek*, 138.

discourse one can not merely add up the semantic content of each colon, since the cola themselves are grouped together by an author to form larger units of material (i.e., paragraphs), which have various semantic functions in the development of the discourse.[7] To understand the semantic program of a main discourse, therefore, one must analyze the relationships between its constituent paragraphs.

Just as cola are grouped to form paragraphs, paragraphs may be grouped to form "embedded discourses," which in turn may be grouped to form larger embedded discourses within the main, or "macro-," discourse.[8] The embedding of discourse subsections within a macro-discourse is depicted in fig. 12.

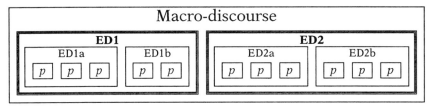

Fig. 12. Discourse embedding within a macro-discourse: ED = embedded discourse; *p* = paragraph.

---

[7] Louw, *The Semantics of New Testament Greek*, 98. Louw states,
Though the colon is the basic unit employed in discourse analysis, the most relevant unit for the explication of the semantic content of a discourse is the paragraph, since it is the largest unit possessing a single unitary semantic scope. The colon, however, is the most convenient starting point for the analysis of a text, since paragraphs are generally too large to handle from the outset.

[8] Linda Neeley states,
Especially in long discourses, paragraphs combine to form sections (cf. [*sic*] chapters in a novel). There is evidence that these sections have their own internal organization that resembles that of a complete discourse; that is, it may have its own introductory paragraph, its paragraphs which develop its theme, and its conclusion. It is, in other words, a smaller discourse embedded in the larger one, an *embedded discourse*. At times, these embedded discourses themselves are quite long and may be divided into their own sections composed of paragraphs (cf. [*sic*] sections in the chapter of a novel). These smaller sections can also be shown to be embedded discourses, having structures similar to that of a complete discourse. As such, they are embedded discourses within an embedded discourse.
Neeley, "A Discourse Analysis of Hebrews," 3.

For example, David Aune's book *The New Testament in its Literary Environment* is a written discourse attempting to discuss various aspects of the literary environment of the New Testament world. His overall discourse is made up of embedded discourses called chapters. The chapter "Luke-Acts and Ancient Historiography" is a self-contained discourse, yet it contributes to the overall theme of the book as a whole.

The embedded discourse "Luke-Acts and Ancient Historiography" is made up of still smaller embedded discourse units such as "The Problem of Genre," "Hellenistic Historiography," and "Comparing Ancient Historiographies." To help the reader Aune has provided "signals" in his work to mark the beginnings of various divisions. The beginning of each chapter is marked with a large number in bold print (e.g. "*1*") followed by the chapter title in large bold letters. The major embedded discourses within each chapter are also bold print with a type face slightly larger than the text itself. The subdivisions of these embedded discourses are marked with an italicized type face the same size as the type face used for the text. Paragraphs, set apart by indention of the first sentence in the paragraph, are the smallest embedded discourse divisions.

Unfortunately, the "signals" which mark the beginnings or endings of units in ancient texts are not as easily recognized by the modern eye. Therefore, through text linguistics the critic attempts to identify unit boundaries in the discourse. Identification of turning points in the development of the author's discussion provides a beginning place for the isolation of units which have various functions in the discourse.

IDENTIFICATION OF UNIT BOUNDARIES

Tracking Cohesion Shifts in the Discourse

The Concept of Cohesion
Cohesion, as used in linguistic investigation, may be defined as a semantic property of a text which gives the text unity.[9] Any dis-

---

[9] The terms "cohesion" and "coherence" are somewhat synonymous. For example, *Webster's II New Riverside University Dictionary* defines *cohesion* as "The act,

course unit has a network of relationships, some grammatical and others lexical, which make that unit of text cohesive.[10] Genre, topic, conjunction, logical relationships between parts of an argument or narrative, consistency of grammatical subject, verb tense, person and number, lexical repetition, consistency of temporal and spatial indicators, or various types of reference all may serve in making a discourse cohesive at the paragraph or embedded discourse level.

Genre
The identification of literary "forms" in the New Testament is possible because such forms display certain consistent characteristics. This consistency provides a unit of text with one type of structural cohesiveness.[11] In the present discussion, the genre will always be either exposition or exhortation, the two prominent genres in the book of Hebrews.

Topic
Although the terms "topic" and "theme" may be used as synonyms, in the present study "topic" is used to refer to the primary message communicated by the group of cola under consideration. A consistent discussion of the same topic, or closely related topics, throughout a unit of material gives the unit a semantic matrix around which the unit coheres.

---

process, or state of cohering." Yet, some linguists have used these words to make distinctions between different dynamics in a discourse. Robert-Alain de Beaugrande and Wolfgang Dressler, for instance, use the term "cohesion" to refer to dynamics on the surface structure of the text, while using "coherence" to refer to dynamics on the notional level. What Klaus Berger, Teun van Dijk, Peter Cotterell and Max Turner refer to as "coherence," is roughly synonymous to the definition of "cohesion" found in M.A.K. Halliday and Ruqaiya Hasan. Use of the term "cohesion" in the present study follows the definition of Halliday and Hasan and may be used interchangeably with the concept of coherence as used by Berger and others. See Robert-Alain de Beaugrande and Wolfgang Dressler, *Introduction to Text Linguistics*, Longman Linguistics Library (New York: Longman, 1981), chap. 4; Berger, *Exegese des Neuen Testaments*, 12-17; Teun van Dijk, *Text and Context* (New York: Longman, 1977), chap. 4; Cotterell and Turner, *Linguistics and Biblical Interpretation*, 230-31.

[10] Halliday and Hasan, *Cohesion in English*, 5-6; Neeley, "A Discourse Analysis of Hebrews," 18-19.

[11] Berger, *Exegese des Neuen Testaments*, 7-8; Gordon D. Fee, *New Testament Exegesis: A Handbook for Students and Pastors* (Philadelphia, PA: The Westminster Press, 1983), 38.

Connection

Connection may be defined in terms of semantic interdependence between two cola. This interdependence conforms to certain constraints which make the relationship between the cola part of an acceptable act of communication. These constraints are semantic and not syntactic (i.e., a sentence may be well-formed grammatically and not make sense) and are not dependent on the presence of connectives (e.g., conjunctions). The cola may be linked by the association of the facts set forth in their propositions. These facts may relate logically, temporally, locally, or by other means.[12] Based on the concept of connection, the question for any individual colon in a unit may be: "What dynamic connects this colon with the one which precedes it, or the one which it precedes?"[13]

Connectives, surface structure expressions which demonstrate some relation between propositions in a discourse, are, however, one means of connection.[14] While conjunctions, sentential adverbs, prepositions with connective character, interjections, and particles may all be considered connectives, the present study will focus on conjunctions and sentential adverbs.

Subject, "actor," verb tense, person, and number

The consistent use of the same subject, the same verb tense, person, or number adds cohesion to a unit of material.[15] In Hebrews, as well as the rest of the New Testament, the subject is often communicated through the verbal form.

In addition, a distinction may be made between the subject of a

---

[12] Van Dijk, *Text and Context*, chaps. 3-4.

[13] This type of analysis is covered by Nida, Louw, and others in *Style and Discourse* under the title "The Meaning of Internuclear Structures" and may also be designated constituent analysis. Cotterell and Turner deal with the relationship between propositions under "Meaning Relations between Pairs of Sentences or Propositions." See Nida, Louw, and others, *Style and Discourse*, 99-105; Cotterell and Turner, *Linguistics and Biblical Interpretation*, 203-17.

[14] Halliday and Hasan, *Cohesion in English*, 226-73. For Halliday and Hasan the designation "conjunction" refers to what has been described above as "connection."

[15] Berger, *Exegese des Neuen Testaments*, 15-16. Speaking of the importance of repetition in building *Kohärenz* in a text Berger states,

> Das wichtigste und vielseitigste Mittel der Textverknüpfung ist die *Wiederholung*. Dasselbe Element wird an verschiedenen Stellen des Textes wiederaufgenommen. Für den Rezipienten ist die Wirkung der Wiederholung integrativ, intensivierend, erweiternd, Aufmerksamkeit weckend (Ibid., 13).

colon and the "actor."[16] The actor in the colon is the originator of some action. For example, in the sentence "Bill cooked the eggs," "Bill" is both the subject of the sentence and the actor. However, in the sentence "The eggs were cooked by Bill," "eggs" is the subject and "Bill" is still the actor. If a certain actor performs action throughout a unit of material, this adds cohesiveness to the unit.

Pronominal Reference

Reference, as used in the present study, may be defined as "the relation between an element of the text and something else by reference to which it is interpreted in the given instance."[17] Reference items may be pronominals (e.g., he, him, his, she, it, their), demonstratives (e.g., this, that, those), the definite article, or comparatives (e.g., same, identical, different).[18] Reference items allow an author to deal with a subject without repeating the same lexical item over and over again. The consistent reference to one or more items throughout a unit provides that unit with cohesiveness.

The analysis below will focus on pronominal reference. As with the subject, pronouns are often communicated through the verbal form in Greek. In the cohesion analysis performed below, the reference item will be identified along with the lexical source, which provides the reader with the information needed to interpret the reference item.

Lexical cohesion

The designation "lexical cohesion" means that cohesion is established through the repetition of similar, or identical, lexical forms, or an association of lexical meanings.[19] Albert Vanhoye's "characteristic terms" are one form of lexical cohesion.[20]

---

[16] Halliday and Hasan, *Cohesion in English*, 310-14.

[17] Ibid., 308.

[18] Ibid., 333-34; Berger, *Exegese des Neuen Testaments*, 15. Berger notes that whole paragraphs may be pronominalized.

[19] To reference and lexical cohesion may be added another kind of relationship between words. Ellipsis is the omission of a word or words necessary to make the statement grammatically complete. The omitted words are, nevertheless, understood via the context. See Nida, Louw, and others, *Style and Discourse*, 33-35; Halliday and Hasan, *Cohesion in English*, 314-18.

[20] Albert Vanhoye, following A. Descamps, set forth "characteristic terms" as one means of discerning the structure of Hebrews. Vanhoye's "characteristic terms" roughly correspond to what is referred to in the present study as "lexical

Two subcategories of lexical cohesion may be identified. *Reiteration* refers to the

> repetition of a lexical item, or the occurrence of a synonym of some kind, in the context of reference; that is, where the two occurrences have the same referent.[21]

For example, the *exempla* of Heb. 11:1-12:3 is built around the repetition of the word πίσει. This is reiteration.

Collocation, on the other hand, may occur when a lexical item is repeated without having the same referent as the previous occurrence of the lexical item. For example, up until Heb. 5:1 the word ἀρχιερεύς has been used to refer to Jesus (2:17, 3:1, 4:14). In Heb. 5:1, however, Jesus is no longer the referent for ἀρχιερεύς. Here the word is used in a more general sense to refer to anyone filling the Old Testament office of high priest. The word ἀρχιερεύς in Heb. 5:1, however, still provides a certain degree of cohesion between 5:1 and the preceding three verses by virtue of lexical identity. This is lexical cohesion by collocation.[22]

Temporal and spatial indicators
The consistent reference to a certain time frame or location provides yet another means of cohesion in a discourse unit. While temporal and local indicators play a much more central role in narrative, they may serve to build temporal and local frames of reference in expositional or hortatory discourse. The temporal frame of reference may be established through nominals which indicate time (e.g., "today," or "friday") or other elements in the context. The spatial frame, may be stated through reference to a certain place (e.g., "in heaven"), or in relation to the speaker (e.g., "here I stand") or hearers (e.g., "you must go out into the world").[23]

---

cohesion." Lexical elements may play a unifying role in individual units of a discourse, but also may span several units, indicating a relationship between those units. See Vanhoye, *La structure littéraire de l'Épître aux Hébreux*, 37.

Related, though not identical, elements may be categorized as follows: (1) those based on similarity, including (a) overlapping relations (proper synonymy), (b) contiguous relations (improper synonymy), and (c) inclusive relations (hyponymy); and (2) those based on oppositeness, including (a) binary relations (antonymy), and (b) multiple relations (incompatibility). See Silva, *Biblical Words and Their Meaning: An Introduction to Lexical Semantics*, 119-36.

[21] Halliday and Hasan, *Cohesion in English*, 318-19.
[22] Ibid., 319.
[23] Cotterell and Turner, *Linguistics and Biblical Interpretation*, 234-39.

"Cohesion Shift" Analysis
Concentration of cohesive dynamics makes the highest level of cohesion in a discourse occur at the paragraph level. Cola of the same paragraph have a higher level of cohesiveness when considered together than with cola outside that paragraph because so many features providing cohesion are brought to bear.[24] The cohesive dynamics provide each paragraph with a unique semantic program. Furthermore, paragraphs of the same embedded discourse have a higher level of cohesiveness when considered together than with paragraphs outside that embedded discourse. This cohesiveness gives distinction to each embedded discourse unit.

In a paragraph, or larger embedded discourse unit, which has a high level of cohesion, there should be relative consistency in most of the "cohesion fields" of genre, topic, subject, actor, verb tense, person, and number, as well as temporal and local frames of reference. A repetition of lexical or reference items may also be present. While shifts in the cohesion fields will occur throughout even the most cohesive discourse unit (e.g., the author may make a change in subject or verb tense) *there should be corresponding shifts in several of the cohesion fields when the discourse moves from one paragraph or embedded discourse to the next.* Corresponding shifts occur because, with the change to a new unit, the cohesive dynamics change. Identification of these corresponding cohesion shifts may be accomplished by careful colon by colon analysis of the text. Such analysis, referred to in the present study as "cohesion shift analysis," offers a beginning point for the delimitation of discourse units by identification of unit boundaries. This approach will constitute the focus of Chapter 4.[25]

Identification of Inclusions

The identification of inclusions offers a second means by which unit boundaries in Hebrews may be isolated. This aspect of analysis will be utilized in Chapter 5 of the present study. As noted under the History of Investigation, the *inclusio* was a commonly used device in ancient literary traditions, clear examples of the device being found in both biblical and extra-biblical sources. Through *inclusio* an

---

[24] So Berger, *Exegese des Neuen Testaments*, 13.
[25] Ibid.

author marked the beginning and ending sections of a block of text with distant lexical parallels. While these parallels may involve the same elements, synonymous or complementary elements may be utilized as well. The elements forming an *inclusio* may reside *near* the beginning or ending of a unit, rather than at the exact initiation or termination points.[26]

In Chapter 5 uses of lexical repetition which could be seen as forming an *inclusio* will be analyzed. If an inclusion is identified, the beginning and ending of the unit marked by the inclusion will be noted as a turning point in the discourse. Therefore, identification of inclusions, an ancient literary device, will be used in conjunction with cohesion shift analysis, a modern linguistic method, in the identification of unit boundaries in Hebrews.

DEMONSTRATING THE INTERRELATEDNESS OF UNITS IN THE DISCOURSE

How Discourse Units May Be Connected

Once units of text have been isolated through identification of their boundaries, the investigation will turn to an examination of how those units interact in the macro-discourse. Demonstration of the interrelatedness of two or more discourse units may be accomplished by identification of (1) inclusions which mark large sections of the discourse, (2) a high degree of lexical and pronominal cohesion between the units, or (3) transition devices used to move from one unit to the next.

Inclusions as Markers of Broader Sections of the Discourse
Inclusions may mark broad sections of a discourse. Their identification may thus be used as one means of isolating *groups* of discourse units which perform a specific semantic program in the discourse.

---

[26] Ball, *A Rhetorical Study of Zephaniah*, 8; Lausberg, *Handbuch der literarischen Rhetorik* 317; Volkmann, *Rhetorik der Griechen und Römer in systematischer Übersicht*, 471; Kennedy, *Interpretation of the New Testament through Rhetorical Criticism*, 34. For its use in biblical literature see Jackson and Kessler, eds., *Rhetorical Criticism: Essays in Honor of James Muilenburg*, 24; Spicq, *L'Épître aux Hébreux*, 31-32. For the use of inclusions in the homiletic pattern discerned by Peder Borgen in John 6 see Borgen's *Bread From Heaven*, 34-38.

This possibility, as it relates to the book of Hebrews, will be investigated at the end of Chapter 5.

Lexical and Pronominal Cohesion Between Units
Uncovering threads of meaning which hold sections of the discourse together, as well as the discourse in its entirety, stands as a primary task of text-linguistic analysis. Semantic threads in a discourse are most often woven with the same, or related, lexical items. Such items may be used repeatedly in two or more units, enhancing the semantic relationship between those units.[27] Therefore, identification of lexical cohesion between units offers an important means of perceiving the relatedness of those units.

For example, in the first two paragraphs of C. H. Dodd's *The Parables of the Kingdom* the word "parable" occurs in both paragraph units:

> The *parables* are perhaps the most characteristic element in the teaching of Jesus Christ as recorded in the Gospels. They have upon them, taken as a whole, the stamp of a highly individual mind, in spite of the rehandling they have inevitably suffered in the course of transmission. Their appeal to the imagination fixed them in the memory, and gave them a secure place in the tradition. Certainly there is no part of the Gospel record which has for the reader a clearer ring of authenticity.
>
> But the interpretation of the *parables* is another matter. Here there is no general agreement. In the traditional teaching of the Church for centuries they were treated as allegories, in which each term stood as a cryptogram for an idea, so that the whole had to be de-coded term by term. A famous example is Augustine's interpretation of the *parable* of the Good Samaritan. [italics mine][28]

In the first paragraph Dodd sets forth a very general statement concerning parables. The semantic program of the second shifts to a consideration of the interpretation of parables. However, use of the term "parable" in both paragraphs keeps the *main* topic in focus for the reader and effects a semantic relationship between the two paragraphs.

---

[27] As a semantic property of discourse, cohesion built through use of lexical items can relate two non-structurally aligned units of text. For example, an author, in the conclusion of a discourse, may make reference to a topic he covered early in the discourse. Through the reference a *semantic* relationship between the two units is established, the hearer or reader being reminded of material that has been covered earlier. This semantic relationship adds cohesiveness to the overall discourse.

[28] C.H. Dodd, *The Parables of the Kingdom* (London: Nisbet & Co., 1935), 11.

Dodd also uses the pronouns "they," "them," and "their" throughout the selection quoted above. These pronouns all refer to the parables of Jesus. Along with lexical cohesion, therefore, these two paragraphs may be said to have *pronominal cohesion*. Pronouns allow an author to deal with a subject without always repeating the same lexical item over and over. Pronoun use plays an important role in enhancing the cohesiveness of either individual units or a group of units in a discourse.

Transition Devices
One of the most neglected topics in discussions on the structure of Hebrews is the author's use of various transition techniques.[29] Transitions effect a special type of lexical cohesion in a discourse.[30] Through transitions an author executes smooth passage from one unit to the next, utilizing important lexical items strategically placed at the beginning, or end of a text unit. Identification of transition techniques in Hebrews offers a third means of discerning the relationship between individual discourse units in the book.

Lexical and pronominal cohesion in Hebrews will be investigated in the first part of Chapter 6. The study will continue with an examination of the special form lexical cohesion takes in the author's transition techniques.

Making Sense of the Macro-discourse

It is not sufficient, however, merely to demonstrate that discourse units relate to other discourse units in the macro-discourse. *Why they are arranged in their present positions* stands as the ultimate question for any structural investigation. In rhetorical criticism the attempt to answer this question is carried out under a consideration of the arrangement of material. Speaking of this step in rhetorical criticism, George Kennedy suggests the critic needs to ask, concerning the text,

---

[29] However, see Neeley, "A Discourse Analysis of Hebrews," 8-10. This neglect, perhaps more than any other factor, accounts for the tremendous diversity in current outlines of Hebrews (supra, 21-23).

[30] Both inclusions and transitions are specialized forms of lexical cohesion in which the lexical items are strategically placed to show the cohesiveness of a section of the discourse (in the case of inclusions) or the movement from one section to the next (in the case of transitions).

what subdivisions it falls into, what the persuasive effect of these parts
seems to be, and how they work together—or fail to do so—to some
unified purpose in meeting the rhetorical situation.[31]

Having identified the embedded discourses in Hebrews, the study
will in Chapter 7 consider the distinct function and arrangement of
those units in the book. Of special concern will be the relationship
between expository and hortatory units of material, a puzzle which
must be addressed in assessing the structure. Chapter 7 will conclude with an attempt at depicting the organization of Hebrews via
an outline.

---

[31] Kennedy, *New Testament Interpretation through Rhetorical Criticism*, 37.

CHAPTER FOUR

COHESION SHIFT ANALYSIS

The aim of the present chapter is to analyze places in Hebrews where corresponding shifts occur in the cohesion fields of genre, topic,[1] spatial indicator, temporal indicator, actor, subject, verb tense, mood, person, and number, reference, and lexical items. The analysis detailed below started with the completion of a table, a sample of which may be seen in fig. 13. A shift in any column is marked by the " > " symbol placed immediately above the information which indicated the shift.[2]

In an attempt to delineate between the intensity levels of various shifts in the discourse, three designations are utilized. Corresponding shifts at which four or less " > " symbols occur are considered a "low-level shift" in the discourse and are not the primary concern of the present chapter. "Median-level shifts" are those where five to seven " > " symbols correspondingly mark development in the discourse. "High-level shifts" represent those turning points in the book which evidence the greatest intensity. These shifts involve corresponding changes marked by eight or more " > " symbols.

The present chapter focuses on identification of the highest-level shifts in Hebrews. These high-level shifts having been discussed in detail, the study will also note the median-level shifts in the book.

---

[1] The "topics" presented in Chapter 4 are provisional and subject to adjustment as the study unfolds.

[2] Shifts in the "genre" column or the "topic" column were marked by a double use of the " > " symbol (i.e., " > > "), rather than a single use of the symbol. A shift in these columns is considered to carry more weight than a shift in any of the others. Elements in the actor, spatial, temporal, verb, subject, reference, and lexical fields of a particular colon serve the execution of the author's immediate topic. Thus the topic field relates to the semantic program carried out through the whole unit. The same may be said for the genre of a unit. Genre has to do with the formal characteristics of the whole unit. The one exception to the above practice involved the use of very distinct forms of a genre. At points the primary genre may remain constant, but a new form be introduced (e.g., the *exempla* of Hebrews 11 continues the hortatory purpose of the previous section, yet takes a very distinct form). In such cases a single " > " was utilized to mark the shift.

Colon	Genre	Topic	Temp.	Actor	Subj.	Verb Tns	V	M	P	N	Refer.	Lexical
1:1–2a	EXPO	God's Word through the Son	past	God	ὁ θεὸς	Aor	A	I	3	S	he (v) → ὁ θεὸς → ἡμῖν → Believer	
2b	EXPO	Description of the Son	past	God	he (vb)	Aor	A	I	3	S	he (v) → ὁ θεὸς → ὃν → υἱῷ	
2c	EXPO	Description of the Son	past	God / Son	he (vb)	Aor	A	I	3	S	οὗ → υἱῷ, he (v) → ὁ θεὸς	
3–4a	EXPO	Description of the Son	past	Son	he (vb)	Aor	A	I	3	S	ὃς → υἱῷ, αὐτοῦ → ὁ θεὸς, αὐτοῦ → υἱῷ	πάντα ⟶, πάντων 2b, ποιησάμενος ἐποίησεν 2b, μεγαλωσύνης idiom for God
4b	EXPO	Description of the Son	past / pres	Son	he (vb)	Pft	A	I	3	S	αὐτοὺς → ἀγγέλων	κεκληρον. ⟶, κληρονο. 2b
5a	EXPO haraz	God's word to the Son	past	God	he (vb)	Aor	A	I	3	S	he (vb) → ὁ θεὸς, μου → ὁ θεὸς, ἐγὼ → ὁ θεὸς, σὺ & σε → υἱῷ	Υἱός ⟶, υἱῷ 2a, ἀγγέλων ⟶, ἀγγέλων 4

υἱῷ ← υἱ ῷ

Fig. 13. Tracking cohesion shifts in discourse.

"HIGH-LEVEL" COHESION SHIFTS IN HEBREWS

The Shift Between Heb. 1:14 and 2:1

Heb. 1:5-14 sets forth the Son's superiority to the angels based on the proclamations made by God concerning the Son.[3] The rabbis, as well as the Qumran sectaries, would at times chain a number of Old Testament texts together using *Stichworten.* These chain quotations, or *haraz* (חרז), were used to give support for a topic under discussion by the quantity of scriptural support given.[4] In Heb. 1:5-14 the author actually presents three pairs of passages, a concluding text (Ps. 110:1 quoted in Heb. 1:13), and the restatement of one of the passages previously quoted in the chain (1:14).[5] The first pair (1:5) concerns sonship, the second (1:6-7) angels, and the third (1:8-12) the eternality of the Son's reign.[6] Ps. 110:1 presents a proclamation of the Son's *Session* at the right hand of God.[7]

In Heb. 2:1 the author changes to the genre of exhortation and a new topic: "The Necessity of Taking God's Word Seriously."[8] The unit found at Heb. 2:1-4 may be divided into two primary parts: (1) the exhortation found in 2:1 and (2) the grounds of the exhortation,

---

[3] Attridge, *The Epistle to the Hebrews,* 50; Michel, *Der Brief an die Hebräer,* 107; Buchanan, *To the Hebrews,* 13-24.

[4] E. Earle Ellis, *Paul's Use of the Old Testament* (Grand Rapids, MI: Baker Book House, 1981), 49-50; Barth, "The Old Testament in Hebrews," 64. The normal pattern in the rabbis was to quote from the Pentateuch and then to string similar passages from the Prophets and the Writings. Ellis notes that Paul does not follow this pattern in his use of *haraz* (Rom. 9-11). Neither does the author of Hebrews, for his texts here are primarily taken from the Psalms. The method is also found in the Qumran literature in their collections of Testimonies.

[5] Heb. 1:5-14 ends with a final contrast between the Son and the angels, referring to the quote in Heb. 1:7 through repeating forms of πνεύματα and λειτουργούς found in that verse.

[6] Cf. R. Koops, "Chains of Contrasts in Hebrews 1," *Biblical Translator* 34 (February 1983): 220-25; J. P. Meier, "Structure and Theology in Heb. 1,1-14," *Biblica* 66 (1985): 168-89; J. W. Thompson, "The Structure and Purpose of the Catena in Heb. 1:5-13," *Catholic Biblical Quarterly* 38 (March 1976): 352-63.

[7] *"Session,"* from the Latin term *sessio,* refers to the posture of being seated. On the use of Psalm 110 in the New Testament see David M. Hay, *Glory at the Right Hand: Psalm 110 in Early Christianity,* Society of Biblical Literature Monograph Series (Cambridge University Press, 1980) and W. R. G. Loader, "Christ at the Right Hand: Psalm 110:1 in the New Testament," *New Testament Studies* 24 (1978): 199-217.

[8] Spicq, *L'Épître aux Hébreux,* 24-28; Lünemann, *Critical and Exegetical Handbook,* 100.

found in 2:2-4.[9] The grounds of the exhortation have their focal point in the rhetorical question πῶς ἡμεῖς ἐκφευξόμεθα τηλικαύτης ἀμελήσαντες σωτηρίας, found in 2:3a. As with the rhetorical questions in 1:5, 1:13, and 1:14, this rhetorical question is semantically equivalent to a proposition. The author here proposes that a person who rejects the word of salvation through the Son will not escape. What is his basis for this assertion?

The rabbis utilized certain norms by which they carried out interpretation.[10] One of these norms, קל וחומר, or *a fortiori*, is an argument from lesser to greater. In other words, what applies in a less important situation certainly applies in a more important situation. In Heb. 2:2-3 the author carries out such an argument.[11] The "lesser" situation is the receiving of God's word through angels under the old covenant. The author appeals to the hearers' knowledge of the Torah, reminding them that the rejection of God's word brought about severe punishment. The "greater" situation is the receiving of the word of salvation through the Son. That there is scriptural precedent for God's punishment in the lesser situation offers a basis for there being even greater punishment if rejection of God's word takes place in the "greater" situation. The rest of the unit, Heb. 2:3b-4, serves to delimit the term σωτηρίας. Thus, Heb. 2:1-4 forms an integrated unit built around an exhortation for the hearers to pay closer attention to what they have heard.

In the actor field the general Christian community is now in view with the use of ἡμᾶς (2:1) as well as the first person plural pronoun expressed through the verb forms παραρυῶμεν and ἐκφευξόμεθα. The infinitive προσέχειν is the subject of 2:1a, shifting from the use of πάντες in 1:14.[12] Although the verb tense remains present the third person plural of εἰσὶν (1:14) changes to third person singular with δεῖ (2:1).

Whereas "God" and "Son" are the primary referents of 1:5-14, the first person plural pronoun, referring to the Christian commun-

---

[9] Cotterell and Turner, *Linguistics and Biblical Interpretation*, 222.

[10] Longenecker, *Biblical Exegesis in the Apostolic Period*, 34-35; Ellis, *Paul's Use of the Old Testament*, 41.

[11] So Buchanan, *To the Hebrews*, xxiv.

[12] On the use of the infinitive as subject when used with δεῖ and other impersonal verbs see James Hope Moulton, ed., *A Grammar of New Testament Greek*, 3 (Edinburgh: T. & T. Clark, 1963), 139.

ity, finds most frequent expression in 2:1-4.[13] Therefore, corresponding cohesion shifts occur at Heb. 2:1 in the genre, topic, actor, subject, verb person, verb number, and reference fields.

The Shift Between Heb. 2:4 and Heb. 2:5

The author moves back to the genre of exposition at Heb. 2:5 and initiates a new topic built around the quote of Ps. 8:4-6: "Subjection of the World to the Son."[14] The negative Οὐ γὰρ ἀγγέλοις ὑπέταξεν τὴν οἰκουμένην τὴν μέλλουσαν may be turned around to state positively his underlying supposition that τὴν οἰκουμένην τὴν μέλλουσαν has been submitted to the Son. Following the quote, the author comments on the last statement of the quote, πάντα ὑπέταξας ὑποκάτω τῶν ποδῶν αὐτοῦ. Pointing especially to the term πάντα, he suggests that nothing has been left outside the lordship of the Son.[15]

The colon which follows in 2:8c presents the contrast νῦν δὲ οὔπω ὁρῶμεν αὐτῷ τὰ πάντα ὑποτεταγμένα. Yet another contrast follows in 2:9, setting forth what the Christian community does see, i.e. Jesus, the one of whom Ps. 8:4-6 speaks. Accordingly, the latter part of Heb. 2:9 concludes the unit's semantic program concerning "submission" by delimiting Ἰησοῦν, identifying him with the αὐτόν of the quote, who was made a little lower than the angels but then crowned with glory and honor.

"God" again is the main actor at 2:5 and the third person singular masculine pronoun inherent in ὑπέταξεν is the subject. The main referents, as was the case in 1:5-14, are "God" and the "Son." The most prominent lexical items lending cohesiveness to 2:5-9 are forms of ὑποτάσσω found at 2:5, 8a, 8b, and 8c.

---

[13] Lexical cohesion in 2:1-4 centers on terms related to "speaking," also a characteristic of 1:5-14. Thus, important lexical links between 2:1-4 and 1:1-14 may be seen in the use of ἀκουσθεῖσιν (2:1) which is related to the verbs of "speaking" in 1:1-14, ἀγγέλων (2:2), forms of λαλέω (2:2, 3b), θεοῦ (2:4), and κυρίου (2:3), which relates to υἱός in that they are both titles for Christ.

[14] Contra James Swetnam, *Jesus and Isaac: A Study of the Epistle to the Hebrews in Light of the Aqedah*, Analecta Biblica, Investigationes Scientificae in Res Biblicas (Rome: Biblical Institute Press, 1981), 138, who sees the Psalm as quoted here referring to man. However, Psalm 8 is tied to Ps. 110:1 in several christological passages in the New Testament. So Michel, *Der Brief an die Hebräer*, 138-39. On the question of whether the author takes this Psalm as messianic from the beginning, or effects a shift to christology with 2:8b, see Ernst Käsemann, *The Wandering People of God: An Investigation of the Letter to the Hebrews*, trans. Roy A. Harrisville and Irving L. Sandberg (Minneapolis, MN: Augsburg Publishing House, 1984), 122-28.

[15] The rabbis would point to the literal sense of a word to support a particular

Thus the shift between Heb. 2:4 and 2:5 is effected in the genre, topic, actor, subject, reference, and lexical cohesion fields.

The Shift Between Heb. 2:9 and Heb. 2:10

At Heb. 2:10 the author continues his expositional treatment but shifts to a new topic. Heb. 2:10-18 has to do with the Son's solidarity with the "sons" through incarnation; the incarnation is a prerequisite for the Son being able to help the sons.[16]

This basic solidarity between the Son and the sons results in an attitude on the part of the Son. He is not ashamed to call them "brothers," an attitude which finds support in the Old Testament (2:12-13). This attitude, combined with the fact that the παιδία shared a common physical existence, led to the Son's act of also taking part in that physical existence (2:14). His motive for doing so was to strip the devil of power and, at the same time, deliver the enslaved.

In Heb. 2:17a the author presents a statement parallel to the earlier αὐτὸς . . . μετέσχεν τῶν αὐτῶν (2:14b), proclaiming ὤφειλεν κατὰ πάντα τοῖς ἀδελφοῖς ὁμοιωθῆναι. As with the earlier proposition, Heb. 2:17a is followed by the motive for effecting the incarnation—that He might become a faithful and merciful high priest.

The temporal field, which had shifted to a present state in 2:8c, returns to the past with Heb. 2:10. In the actor field the Christian community, briefly reintroduced at 2:8c-9, has been replaced with "God" in 2:10, though "the Son" stands as the main actor lending cohesion to the whole of 2:10-18. The subject field, occupied by the first person plural pronoun expressed through βλέπομεν in 2:9, shifts at 2:10, the infinitive τελειῶσαι taking the subject slot at that point.[17] A shift from the present indicative first plural to the aorist indicative third singular marks the verb columns.

References to "the Son" and "God" have been joined by those to

---

argument. See Longenecker, *Biblical Exegesis in the Apostolic Period*, 28-32; Dan Cohn-Sherbok, "Paul and Rabbinic Exegesis," *Scottish Journal of Theology* 35 (1982): 119.

[16] Bruce, *The Epistle to the Hebrews*, 42-53; Attridge, *The Epistle to the Hebrews*, 78-79.

[17] Note, however, that the first person plural masculine pronoun dominates the subject field of 2:10-18.

"the sons" at 2:10, 11a, 11b, and 15. In the lexical field terms related to family relationships (i.e., υἱός, ἀδελφός, παιδία) predominate, lexical cohesion also being afforded by items related to suffering and death.

Thus a high-level cohesion shift occurs at Heb. 2:10, contributed to in the topic, temporal, actor, subject, verb tense, verb person, verb number, reference, and lexical fields.

The Shift Between Heb. 2:18 and Heb. 3:1

The next high-level cohesion shift occurs at Heb. 3:1, the author moving once again to the genre of exhortation, which he will maintain to the end of Hebrews 4. Whereas the relationship between the Son and the sons was in focus in 2:10-18, the topic now is "Consider Jesus' Superior Faithfulness."

As with Heb. 2:1-4, the unit found at Heb. 3:1-6 may be divided into two primary sections—an exhortation (3:1-2) and the grounds upon which the author bases his exhortation (3:3-6). The hearers are exhorted to consider Jesus, especially keeping in mind his faithfulness, which is comparable to the faithfulness of the great old covenant figure Moses.[18] The discourse continues with the grounds upon which the exhortation stands. The assertion is made that Jesus should be the object of special consideration πλείονος γὰρ οὗτος δόξης παρὰ Μωϋσῆν ἠξίωται.[19]

As already mentioned above, the Son is the primary actor in 2:10-18. Yet this column shows a shift at 3:1 to the Christian community being addressed, the imperative second plural κατανοήσατε encouraging the hearers to action. At 3:1 the subject changes from the "he" of 2:18 to "you" inherent in the imperative verb form.

---

[18] Mary Rose D'Angelo, *Moses in the Letter to the Hebrews*, Society of Biblical Literature Dissertation Series (Missoula, MT: Scholars Press, 1979), 91-92; Weiss, *Handbuch über den Brief an die Hebräer*, 88-98.

[19] This proclamation of Jesus' superior worthiness finds expansion in two directions. First, the author draws an analogy between Jesus' relationship to Moses and a builder's relationship to a house he has built (3:3b-4). The inference to which the analogy points is that Jesus, as God, has made Moses, and thus, as creator, is worthy of greater honor than one of his creatures. In this regard see Heb. 1:2 and 1:10, which speak of the Son's role in creation of the world.

Second, that Jesus is worthy of more glory than Moses finds support in a *contrast* between the respective, earthly roles each lived out in faithfulness to God. Moses was faithful ὡς θεράπων, while Christ was faithful ὡς υἱός.

References to the Son and to God are joined by references to the Christian community. The terms Ἰησοῦν and Χριστός designate the Son. These designations, along with the lexical item Μωϋσῆς and use of the term πιστόν, add cohesiveness in the lexical column.

The Shifts at Heb. 3:6 and Heb. 3:12

Two high-level cohesion shifts occur in the rest of Hebrews 3, one at Heb. 3:7, and another at 3:12.[20] Both shifts are due to the extensive quote at 3:7-11, which is introductory to what follows. The somewhat complex exhortation of Heb. 3:7-4:2 is built around the negative example of those who, through their disobedience to God, fell in the wilderness, failing to enter the promised rest.[21] Broadly speaking, this section falls into an introduction (3:7-11), an exhortation (3:12-14), elaboration of the central motif communicated by the introduction (3:15-19), and a concluding exhortation (4:1-2).[22]

At Heb. 3:7, the temporal frame of reference remains present and the verb form changes to present subjunctive second person plural. In the actor column the emphasis returns to the hearers, and the subject correspondingly shifts to the second person plural pronoun contained in the verb form.

References to the Son, for the first time in the discourse, are conspicuously absent in 3:7-4:2, while those referring to God and the Christian community are joined by references to the "wander-

---

[20] In Heb. 3:7-8 σκληρύνητε is the central matrix of the colon, the author using the words of Psalm 95 as his own words to exhort his listeners.

[21] Many commentators, however, end the immediate section with Heb. 3:19. So Montefiore, *A Commentary on the Epistle to the Hebrews*, 80; and Michel, *Der Brief an die Hebräer*, 190-91.

[22] Several of the concepts contained in Heb. 3:12-4:2, though absent from Psalm 95, find expression in other "rebellion in the wilderness" pericopes of the Old Testament. In Heb. 3:16-18, the questions at the beginning of each verse are taken directly from the quote of Ps. 95:8-11. The answers provided, however, are not found in that pericope. That it was those who came out of Egypt with Moses who provoked the Lord in the wilderness (Heb. 3:16) does find expression in Ps. 106, Num. 14:1-38, and Deut. 9. That it was those who sinned, whose bodies fell in the wilderness, with whom God was angry (Heb. 3:17) is also found in Ps. 106 (vv. 6,26) and Num. 14:1-38. Finally, the concept of disobedience (utilizing the term ἀπειθέω) is found in Deut. 9:7,24.

Furthermore, the author of Hebrews suggests those in the wilderness failed to enter the promised land because of a failure to believe (3:12,19, 4:2). This important motif finds expression in Deut. 9:23, Num. 14:11, and Ps. 78:22,32.

ers" in the wilderness. The quote at 3:7-11 provides the lexical base for 3:7-4:2, lexical cohesion being built especially through terms related to "heart," "day," "today," "harden," "enter in," "belief," "rest," and "hear his voice." With the references to "entering in" cohesion builds in the spatial column.

The Shift Between Heb. 4:2 and Heb. 4:3

Whereas the hazard of "falling short" through "unbelief" stands as the primary topic of Heb. 3:7-4:2, the topic shifts in 4:3-11 to a promised "rest" which may still be entered through "belief." The transition is effected, in part, by the author's use of גזירה שׁוה, a rabbinic method of interpretation based on verbal analogy.[23] Still playing off Ps. 95:7c-11, he quotes Gen. 2:2, the joining of the latter to the former based on the cognates κατάπαυσιν (Ps. 95:11) and κατέπαυσεν (Gen. 2:2).

Setting forth the verbal analogy between Ps. 95:11 and Gen. 2:2, the author argues that there is indeed a rest which, though first spoken of in relation to the creation of the world and still operable at the time of the wilderness wanderings, was not entered into by those in the wilderness (4:3-6).[24] He then uses the word σήμερον (Ps. 95:7c) and points out that God, speaking through David years after the wilderness wanderings, mentions "another day" in relation to His promised rest (4:7-8). For the author, the term σήμερον shows that God's rest was, in David's day, (and is) still promised to God's people.[25]

At Heb. 4:3 the change in topic is accompanied by a shift in the actor field to the first person plural pronoun communicated in the verbal form. Correspondingly, the actor field shifts to the "Christian community" to whom the pronoun refers. Also, the temporal field changes from past to present, and the verb shifts from aorist third singular to present first plural.

---

[23] For further explanation of this method see Ellis, *Paul's Use of the Old Testament*, 41; Kistemaker, *The Psalm Citations in the Epistle to the Hebrews*, 71.

[24] On the promised rest see Windisch, *Der Hebräerbrief*, 34-35.

[25] Attridge, *The Epistle to the Hebrews*, 130-31.

The Shift Between Heb. 4:11 and Heb. 4:12

The beautifully constructed warning of Heb. 4:12-13 deals with the power of God's word and the impossibility of hiding from his judgment. An ellipsis marks the verb fields at 4:12, although the present indicative third person singular is understood. The λόγος is both the subject of the colon and the main actor. Also, the temporal frame of reference shifts from a future frame of reference to a "gnomic," or timeless, frame in 4:12.[26] Therefore, at Heb. 4:12 corresponding shifts occur in the topic, actor, temporal, subject, and verb fields.

The Shift Between Heb. 4:13 and Heb. 4:14

Although the genre remains exhortation, the topic shifts at Heb. 4:14 to "Jesus' High Priesthood: the Basis for Right Action." The cola of 4:14-16 cluster around two conjoined exhortations: (1) κρατῶμεν τῆς ὁμολογίας (14b), and (2) προσερχώμεθα . . . τῷ θρόνῳ (16a). Each exhortation follows a statement of facts offered as its grounds. The second exhortation alone is trailed by a motive: ἵνα λάβωμεν ἔλεος καὶ χάριν εὕρωμεν εἰ εὔκαιρον βοήθειαν.

The temporal field reverts from the gnomic frame of 4:12-13, and the spatial field shifts to movement "through the heavens." The Christian community once again finds its place in the actor slot with 4:14, replacing the "being" orientation of 4:13. The present subjunctive first person plural κρατῶμεν shows a shift in the verb mood, person, and number columns, and provides a shift in subject to the first person plural pronoun expressed in the verb form.

The Shift Between Heb. 4:16 and Heb. 5:1

A high-level cohesion shift may be discerned at Heb. 5:1 by noting corresponding shifts in the genre, topic, temporal, actor, subject, verb, and reference fields. Here the author finally breaks with the

---

[26] The gnomic perspective is "used in generalizations or proverbs." See Moulton, ed., *A Grammar of New Testament Greek*, 3, 63.

This phenomenon is also referred to by Dana and Mantey as the "static." See H. E. Dana and Julius Mantey, *A Manual Grammar of the Greek New Testament* (Toronto: The Macmillan Company, 1957), 186. The static state is defined as "a condition which is assumed as perpetually existing, or to be ever taken for granted as fact."

exhortation initiated at 3:1 and turns again to the genre of exposition. The topic, although not unrelated to that of 4:14-16, changes to "Appointment to the Office of High Priest," the author first dealing with the appointment of high priests in general (5:1-4), and then the appointment of Christ to that office (5:5-10).[27]

The temporal frame of reference shifts again to a gnomic framework at Heb. 5:1. The actor in this first verse of chapter 5 is not quite clear. However, the parallel passage in Heb. 7:26-28 suggests the author may, in 5:1, have "the Law" in mind as the appointing agent. Nevertheless, a shift occurs from the Christian community, the actors in 4:14-16. The new subject in 5:1 is ἀρχιερεύς and the verb shifts from present subjunctive first plural (4:16) to present indicative third singular. In the reference field the high priest is the constant item referred to through 5:4, changing from the references to the Christian community in 4:14-16.

The Shift Between Heb. 5:10 and Heb. 5:11

Changing again to hortatory material, with Heb. 5:11 the author confronts his hearers concerning their spiritual immaturity.[28] Heb. 5:11-6:3 sets forth the problem (5:11-14) followed by an exhortation to move on to maturity (6:1-3). A temporal orientation to past events, found in Heb. 5:5-10, gives way to consideration of the present circumstance.

The construction πολὺς . . . ὁ λόγος was a common literary idiom for "there is much to say."[29] Thus the reader is left with an ellipsis, which produces shifts in the verb columns. The actor column may, however, be filled with the implied "speaker." While the appropriate item for the subject column is questionable, the statement of 5:11 definitely represents a shift from the subject of the previous colon. As to the referents in Heb. 5:11-6:3, the speaker and the hearers are most common through Heb. 6:3.

---

[27] Héring, L'Épître aux Hébreux, 51-52; Spicq, L'Épître aux Hébreux, 106-109.

The smooth transition between 4:14-16 and 5:1 is executed by the common use of ἀρχιερεύς. This term provides lexical cohesion by collocation, rather than reiteration, since the term as used in 4:14-16 has a different referent than the use in 5:1. In Heb. 5:1 the author moves to a more global use referring to anyone at any time filling the office of high priest.

[28] Michel, Der Brief an die Hebräer, 230; Brooke Foss Westcott, The Epistle to the Hebrews: The Greek Text with Notes and Essays (London: MacMillan, 1929), 130-31.

[29] Moffatt, A Critical and Exegetical Commentary on the Epistle to the Hebrews, 69.

The Shift Between Heb. 6:3 and Heb. 6:4

One of the most controversial passages in the book, Heb. 6:4-8 offers a severe warning to those of the Christian community who would fall away from the salvation experienced through Christ.[30] The author speaks of the impossibility of renewing those to repentance who, having once tasted the blessings of God, reject those blessings. His warning is reinforced by the agricultural analogy of Heb. 6:7-8.

Beginning at 6:4 the gnomic marks the temporal frame. Although ellipsis dominates the verb fields, a present indicative third person singular ("it is") is probably to be understood. The infinitive ἀνα-καινίζειν stands as the subject, a construction making the actor of the passage unclear. In the reference field Heb. 6:4 shows a shift to "those who have fallen away" as the primary referents. Therefore, the high-level cohesion shift following Heb. 6:3 is carried out in the topic, temporal, verb, subject, and reference fields.

The Shift Between Heb. 6:8 and Heb. 6:9

Heb. 6:9-12 follows the severe warning of 6:4-8 with mitigation, expressing confidence that the hearers stand outside the group to which his warning applies. This change in topic joins shifts in the actor, temporal, verb tense, verb person, verb number, subject, and reference fields. The first person plural pronoun communicated through the verb once again sets forth the speaker as actor and provides the subject of the colon. The temporal frame reverts from the gnomic idea of 6:4-8. In the verb fields Heb. 6:9 sees a shift to the perfect first person plural with Πεπείσμεθα. The Christian community being addressed and the speaker himself are the most common referents.

The Shift Between Heb. 6:12 and Heb. 6:13

With Heb. 6:13 the author begins to address the topic "God's Oath."[31] The author shows the certainty of God's promise by quoting Gen. 22:17, Εἰ μὴν εὐλογῶν εὐλογήσω σε καὶ πληθύνων πληθυνῶ,

---

[30] Buchanan, *To the Hebrews*, 105-111; Attridge, *The Epistle to the Hebrews*, 166-67.

[31] Lünemann, *The Epistle to the Hebrews*, 248-57; Montefiore, *A Commentary on the Epistle to the Hebrews*, 112-17.

Abraham being presented as a paradigm of one who patiently wait-
ed for the sure outcome (6:13-15). The fact of God's dependability
once he has made a promise is offered for the hearer's encouragement (6:16-20).

With the discussion of Abraham at Heb. 6:13-15, the author
moves the discussion to a past temporal frame for the first time since
5:10. Here, in 6:13, God is the actor, ὁ θεός also functioning as the
subject of the colon. Also, with this verse the verb columns change
to aorist indicative third singular. "God" also is the main referent
through v. 17, a change from references to the Christian community
which are predominant in 6:9-12.

The Shift Between Heb. 6:20 and Heb. 7:1

The genre of exposition begins afresh with Heb. 7:1, where the
author enters into the topic "The Greatness of Melchizedek."[32]
While the spatial orientation to "entrance within the veil" of 6:19-
20 shifts with 7:1-3, the temporal frame of the latter seems to change
to present, resting most squarely on the main verb μένει. Μελχισέδεκ is both the main actor and the subject at the beginning of
Hebrews 7, causing a shift from Ἰησοῦς in 6:20. The verb tense also
changes from aorist to present.

Melchizedek stands as the primary referent in 7:1-10, a change
from the references to the Christian community at the end of Hebrews 6. A high level of lexical cohesion is also built in 7:1-10 especially through the terms Μελχισέδεκ, Αβραάμ, and ἱερεύς.

The Shift Between Heb. 10:18 and Heb. 10:19

While a number of median-level shifts occur throughout Hebrews
7-10, the next high-level shift comes with Heb. 10:19. At 10:19
discussion of "The Finality of Christ's Sacrifice," explicated in 10:1-
18, gives way before the fresh exhortation to take action on the basis
of Christ's superior priesthood. Along with this shift in topic and
genre come the hortatory use of the present subjunctive first person
plural form of the verb and, as subject, the first person plural pro-

---

[32] Michel, *Der Brief an die Hebräer*, 255-63; Riggenbach, *Der Brief an die Hebräer*,
176-215. On the midrashic style of Hebrews 7 see J. A. Fitzmyer, "'Now this
Melchizedek' (Heb. 7:1)" *Catholic Biblical Quarterly* 25 (1963): 305-21.

noun expressed in that verbal form. Correspondingly the actor column is filled by the "Christian community," the members of which
are the primary referents in 10:19-39. The spatial column shows a
renewed emphasis on entrance into the heavenly holy of holies,
especially expounded in Hebrews 9.

The Shift Between Heb. 10:39 and Heb. 11:1

Although the author continues to exhort his hearers in Hebrews 11,
the form to which that exhortation conforms is known as *exempla*.[33]
This form of the exhortation genre provides a high level of cohesion
in the eleventh chapter of Hebrews and, thus, has significant bear-
ing on the cohesion fields of that section. For example, the constant
repetition of πίστει throughout the chapter now stands as the most
significant element in the lexical field and provides the semantic
basis for the new topic: "The Heroes Who Endured by Faith." The
term πίστις is also the subject of the first colon of Hebrews 11, a
change from ἡμεῖς of the previous colon. Also, the various heroes of
great πίστις have become the main referents with this section.

While the primary temporal frame giving cohesiveness to the
eleventh chapter is past, the shift at 11:1 is from present (10:39) to a
timeless frame of reference (11:1). The verb form also changes from
first person plural to third person singular.

The Shift Between Heb. 12:2 and Heb. 12:3

Continuing with his exhortation, at Heb. 12:3 the author shifts from
his emphasis on faith to focus on a new, though related, topic—
"The Discipline of True Sons." Here the author confronts his listeners with the value of their sonship, even though that status involves
discipline.[34]

---

[33] The formulation of lists of *exempla* to prove or illustrate an author's point finds
expression in a number of different types of ancient literature. Although these lists
are greatly diverse in expression, their common function seems to be "to persuade
people by making the *exempla* they cite appear to be representative of a great many
more that could also be provided as evidence." See Cosby, "The Rhetorical Composition of Hebrews 11," 268.
[34] Michel makes the break here between 11:40 and 12:1; Bruce between 12:3 and
12:4; Spicq between 12:4 and 12:5. See Michel, *Der Brief an die Hebräer*, 425; Bruce,
The Epistle to the Hebrews, 354-55; Spicq, *L'Épître aux Hébreux*, 390-91.

At Heb. 12:3 the temporal frame of reference moves to the present. The verb form shifts to aorist imperative second person plural. The new subject is the second person plural pronoun reflected in that verbal form. The hearers become the primary referents with 12:3 and following, as well as the main actors of 12:3-8.

The Shift Between Heb. 12:17 and Heb. 12:18

Another high-level shift in Hebrews 12 occurs at 12:18. Beginning with this verse and carrying through Heb. 12:24, the author paints a picture of contrast, setting his hearers over against those who wandered in the wilderness under the old covenant.[35] Thus the topic may be stated as "The Contrast Between Old and New Covenant Wanderers." Departing from a past temporal frame surrounding the description of Esau in 12:16-17, the author focuses on a present state which has resulted from the hearers' past action. The author uses the perfect second person plural form of the verb, προσεληλύθατε, to communicate the subject of the colon.

The verb προσέρχομαι, in addition, has an impact on the spatial frame of reference, the emphasis shifting to the wilderness-wandering motif. As is the case with most of the rest of Hebrews 12, the hearers are the primary actors, a shift from Esau as the actor at the end of 12:17. Thus the shift between Heb. 12:17 and 12:18 is executed via the topic, temporal, spatial, actor, subject, verb tense, verb person, and verb number cohesion fields.

The Shift Between Heb. 12:29 and Heb. 13:1

An obvious change in tone occurs with Heb. 13:1.[36] The stern warning of 12:25-29 has been replaced with a text-book example of Dibelius' *paraenesis*.[37] Accordingly, the topic of this new section may be

---

[35] Attridge, *The Epistle to the Hebrews*, 372-77.

[36] So Floyd Filson, '*Yesterday*': *A Study of Hebrews in the Light of Chapter 13*, Studies in Biblical Theology (Naperville, IL: Alec R. Allenson, 1967), 13-14.

[37] Dibelius defined paraenesis as

a text which strings together admonitions of general ethical content. Paraenetic sayings ordinarily address themselves to a specific (though perhaps fictional) audience, or at least appear in the form of a command or summons.

Martin Dibelius, *James: A Commentary on the Epistle of James*, trans. Michael A. Williams, Hermeneia (Philadelphia, PA: Fortress Press, 1976), 3.

put as "General Exhortations." While the temporal frame of reference remains present, the verb form has changed to a present imperative second plural. The hearers once again constitute the main actors as well as the main referents. The second person plural pronoun expressed in the verb form now provides the subject.

The Shifts at Heb. 13:20 and Heb. 13:22

The benediction of Heb. 13:20-21 causes a high-level cohesion shift at 13:20 and again at 13:22. This benediction has God as the main actor, the subject of the colon, and one of the main referents. It separates two passages in which the speaker is the main actor, and the first person singular pronoun reflected in the verb is the main subject. In addition to the obvious change in genre, a corresponding change in topic at 13:20 and again at 13:22 confronts the reader. These two points in the book also present fluctuations in the verb cohesion fields.

"MEDIAN-LEVEL" COHESION SHIFTS IN HEBREWS

In addition to the high-level shifts delineated above, numerous median-level cohesion shifts occur throughout the discourse. Median-level shifts in Hebrews may be found at Heb. 1:5, 3:19, 5:5, 6:1, 6:10, 6:18, 7:11, 7:26, 8:1, 8:3, 8:4, 8:6, 8:7, 9:1, 9:6, 9:11, 9:24, 10:1, 10:5, 10:11, 10:26, 10:32, 11:32, 12:1, 12:9, 12:11, 12:12, 12:14, 12:25, 13:4b, 13:8, 13:9, and 13:18.

SUMMARY

The analysis of what here have been designated as "high-" and "median-level" cohesion shifts in the book of Hebrews has revealed twenty-two high-level shifts and thirty-three median-level shifts in the discourse. That the intensity of the "median-level" shifts is lower than that of the "high-level" shifts, does not necessarily mean all median-level shifts are less significant than all high-level shifts. Also, some median-level shifts may be much more important than others. The significance of the varying degrees of intensity must be evaluated through text-linguistic analysis of the macro-discourse.

    The aim of the present chapter has been to demonstrate that identifiable, corresponding shifts in various dynamics which make a

unit of text cohesive may be tracked throughout the book of Hebrews. This enterprise has been based on one aspect of modern
text-linguistic theory. In Chapter 5 the study considers the author's
use of an ancient literary device, the *inclusio*, to determine if the
author's own marking of his discourse corresponds with the findings
gleaned through cohesion shift analysis.

CHAPTER FIVE

THE AUTHOR'S USES OF *INCLUSIO* IN HEBREWS

More than any other scholar Albert Vanhoye has attempted to use the detection of inclusions as a cornerstone of his literary analysis of the book of Hebrews. By the time the second edition of *La structure littéraire de l'Épître aux Hébreux* reached the press, Vanhoye had found over thirty cases where, he suggested, the author marks the text by *inclusio*. In an article published three years later he would make several adjustments to the list.[1]

A number of Vanhoye's insights are noteworthy. It is the position of this writer, however, that Vanhoye misses key uses of *inclusio* in Hebrews, and at a number of points mistakenly sees inclusions where the author was merely making use of common lexical repetition. Vanhoye seems to err most often when he finds an *inclusio* built around a single word, or short phrase, the special structural function of which may be called into question.[2]

---

[1] Vanhoye, *La structure littéraire de l'Épître aux Hébreux*, 37-52, 222-23, 274-303; idem, "Literarische Struktur und theologische Botschaft," 139-41.

[2] The following "inclusions" noted by Vanhoye in his monograph and the article "Literarische Struktur und theologische Botschaft" (pp. 139-41) may be labeled questionable: use of ἀγγέλων and υἱός at 1:5,6 [vv. 6 and 7 are structurally joined by the *Stichwort* ἀγγέλων]; ἀγγέλοις at 2:5,16; ὑπέταξεν at 2:5,8; εἰσελθεῖν εἰς τὴν κατάπαυσιν at 4:1,5 [terms used throughout those verses]; εἰσελθεῖν and ἀπείθειαν at 4:6,11; προσενέγκῃ at 8:3, 9:28; λειτουργός at 8:2,6; κατεσκευάσθη at 9:2,6; λατρείας at 9:6,9; διαθήκης at 9:15,17; αἵματος at 9:18,22; προσφέρουσιν and προσφορά at 10:1,18 and 10:1,10 and 10:11,14; and "offering for" ἁμαρτίας at 10:11,18; ἐνιαυτόν at 10:1,3; προσφορὰν and σῶμα at 10:5,10; ἁμαρτιῶν at 10:17,18; υἱοῖς at 12:5,8; ἐνετρεπόμεθα and τροχιάς . . . ἐκτραπῇ at 12:9,13; Εἰρήνην and κύριον at 12:14, 13:20; χάριτος and χάριν at 12:15,28.

Vanhoye's identification of inclusions at 1:2,4; 4:12,13; 7:1,3; 7:4,9; 7:26,28; 10:27,31; 11:1,7; 11:23,27; and 13:7,18 may be accurate, yet may simply represent uses of lexical cohesion in those sections of the book.

James Swetnam has criticized Vanhoye's use of *inclusio* as a primary formal criterion for discerning structure. See Swetnam, "Form and Content in Hebrews 1-6," 374. My criticism of Vanhoye differs from that of Swetnam. As demonstrated in the present chapter, inclusions do play a primary role in marking sections of Hebrews. It is not that Vanhoye uses a faulty criterion; it is that he, at points, misuses a vitally important one.

It may be suggested that where a single word, or brief phrase, is identified as the key element utilized to close out an *inclusio*, there should be no intervening use of that word, or the use of that word should be uniquely complementary to the opening, serving to round off the topic under discussion.

HEB. 1:5 AND 1:13

Setting up the *haraz* of Heb. 1̄:5-14, the author asks a rhetorical question concerning the angels and then quotes Ps. 2:7. A close approximation of the same question, complemented by a quotation of Ps. 110:1, stands near the end of the *haraz*.

> Τίνι γὰρ εἶπέν ποτε τῶν ἀγγέλων . . . (+ a quote) (1:5)
>
> τίνα δὲ τῶν ἀγγέλων εἴρηκέν ποτε . . . (+ a quote) (1:13)
>
> Fig. 14. The *inclusio* bracketing the *haraz* of Heb. 1:5-14.

These statements clearly form an *inclusio* marking the beginning and ending of the *haraz*.[3] Heb. 1:14 participates with the rest of the *haraz* in setting forth a contrast between the Son and the angels. The statement in 1:14 may be understood to refer to the quote in Heb. 1:7, repeating forms of πνεύματα and λειτουργούς found in that verse.[4] As such Heb. 1:14 completes the immediate contrast between the Son and the angels, providing one final statement concerning the inferiority of the latter.

The opening of this *inclusio* at Heb. 1:5 corresponds to the median-level cohesion shift noted at that verse. The closing of the *inclusio* corresponds to the high-level cohesion shift found following 1:14.

HEB. 2:10 AND 2:17-18

At least four aspects of Heb. 2:10 are echoed in 2:17-18.

First, the term Ἔπρεπεν in verse 10 roughly corresponds to ὤφειλεν in verse 17.[5] In both cases the necessity, or appropriateness,

---

[3] So Vanhoye, *La structure littéraire de l'Épître aux Hébreux*, 74.
[4] *Supra*, 61.
[5] Swetnam, *Jesus and Isaac*, 130-31.

of an aspect of the incarnation is set forth. Second, in both passages the author presents the Son's "development." In 2:10 the Son is "perfected" (τελειῶσαι) and in 2:17 he "becomes" (γένηται) a merciful and faithful high priest. Third, in both passages he aids the "sons" (v. 10), or "brothers" (v. 17), who are the objects of salvation. Finally, the perfection of the Son (v. 10) and his becoming high priest (v. 17) both involved his suffering (παθημάτων in v. 10; πέπονθεν in v. 18).

Based on these parallels, 2:10 and 2:17-18 may be noted as the opening and closing of an *inclusio* marking the section which runs from 2:10-18. The isolation of the unit in this fashion corresponds to the high-level cohesion shifts found at 2:10 and 3:1. Also, the tail boundary of the section finds further support from an *inclusio* at 3:1/4:14.

HEB. 3:1 AND 4:14

Albert Vanhoye correctly notes an *inclusio*, opened in Heb. 3:1 and closed in 4:14, which is crafted around four terms common to both verses: "Jesus" ('Ιησοῦν), "high priest" (ἀρχιερέα), forms of "heaven" (ἐπουρανίου in 3:1 and οὐρανούς in 4:14), and "confession" (ὁμολογίας).[6] That the *inclusio* opens at 3:1 supplies further evidence that a structural boundary exists between Heb. 2:18 and 3:1. The tail boundary of the section running from 3:1-4:14, however, presents a problem. The question arises whether a sharp division exists between 4:14 and 4:15, as Vanhoye suggests, or whether the section should be seen as running all the way through 4:16. Again, the closing element of an *inclusio* need not occur at the very end of the unit which it marks. This question will be discussed further under a consideration of the *inclusio* at 4:14-16/10:19-23.

HEB. 3:12 AND 3:19

At Heb. 3:12 the author states, Βλέπετε, ἀδελφοί, μήποτε ἔσται ἔν τινι ὑμῶν καρδία πονηρὰ ἀπιστίας . . . Having exhorted the hearers (3:12-15) and then expounded on the peril of those who fell in the wilderness (3:15-18), he then, in 3:19, gives a summary of the latter, commenting καὶ βλέπομεν ὅτι οὐκ ἠδυνήθησαν εἰσελθεῖν δι᾽ ἀπισ-

---

[6] Vanhoye, *La structure littéraire de l'Épître aux Hébreux*, 54.

τίαν. The terms βλέπετε and ἀπιστίας of 3:12 are thus repeated at 3:19.[7] The closing of the unit at verse 19 corresponds to the median-level shift following that verse.

HEB. 4:3 AND 4:11

An *inclusio*, opened with Heb. 4:3 and closed at 4:11, corresponds to two high-level shifts noted in Chapter 4 of the present study.[8] As discussed in that chapter, with Heb. 4:3 the discourse turns to address the reward of rest for those who believe.[9] The author opens the discussion with εἰσερχόμεθα γὰρ εἰς [τὴν] κατάπαυσιν οἱ πιστεύσαντες . . . He closes at Heb. 4:11 stating, σπουδάσωμεν οὖν εἰσελθεῖν εἰς ἐκείνην τὴν κατάπαυσιν.

HEB. 4:14-16 AND 10:19-23

The series of parallels found in 4:14-16 and 10:19-23, noted by Wolfgang Nauck, represent the most striking use of *inclusio* in the book of Hebrews.[10] That Albert Vanhoye has failed to deal with such obvious parallels remains a glaring weakness in his approach to the structure of the book. These parallels, depicted in fig. 15, show that believers have a priest (4:14, 10:21) named "Jesus" (4:14, 10:19), who has led the way into the heavenly realm (4:14, 10:19),[11] and that they should, therefore, hold fast to their confession (4:14, 10:23) and draw near to God (4:16, 10:22).

4:14-16	*10:19-31*
ἔχοντες οὖν ἀρχιερέα μέγαν	ἔχοντες οὖν . . . ἱερέα μέγαν
διεληλυθότα τ. οὐρανούς	. . . διὰ τοῦ καταπετάσματος
Ἰησοῦν τὸν υἱὸν τοῦ θεοῦ	ἐν τῷ αἵματι Ἰησοῦ
κρατῶμεν τῆς ὁμολογίας	κατέχωμεν τὴν ὁμολογίαν
προσερχώμεθα . . . μετὰ παρρησίας . . .	προσεχώμεθα μετὰ ἀληθινῆς καρδίας . . .

Fig. 15. Wolfgang Nauck's assessment of parallels in Heb. 4:14-16 and 10:19-23.

---

[7] Ibid., 95.
[8] Contra Vanhoye who sees inclusions marking 4:1-5 and 4:6-11. Ibid., 96-97.
[9] Supra, 67.
[10] Nauck, "Zum Aufbau des Hebräerbriefes," 200-203.
[11] Εἴσοδον τῶν ἁγίων refers to the heavenly Holy Place (Heb. 9:23-24), the place where Jesus offered his offering before sitting down at the right hand of God (10:10-14).

It may be suggested that slight alterations in Nauck's identification of parallels provide additional insights into the relationship between the two passages. These alterations are depicted in fig. 16.

First, the lead phrase, Ἔχοντες οὖν . . ., may be depicted as a separate correspondence. Second, Nauck failed to mark the parallel relationship between uses of τοῦ θεοῦ, found in both passages. In 4:14 the reference is to the τὸν υἱὸν τοῦ θεοῦ and in 10:21, τὸν οἶκον τοῦ θεοῦ. Third, Nauck also missed the parallel uses of παρρησία. Finally, the parallels in the two passages run only through verse 23 of chapter 10. Therefore, Nauck's extension of the passage to verse 31 at this point seems unwarranted.[12]

4:14-16	*10:19-23*
ἔχοντες οὖν . . .	ἔχοντες οὖν . . .
ἀρχιερέα μέγαν	ἱερέα μέγαν
διεληλυθότα τ. οὐρανούς	. . . διὰ τοῦ καταπετάσματος
Ἰησοῦν	Ἰησοῦ
τὸν υἱὸν τοῦ θεοῦ	τὸν οἶκον τοῦ θεοῦ
κρατῶμεν τῆς ὁμολογίας	κατέχωμεν τὴν ὁμολογίαν
προσερχώμεθα . . . μετά	προσεχώμεθα μετά
παρρησίας	παρρησίαν

Fig. 16. Further identification of parallels in Heb. 4:14-16 and 10:19-23.

The *inclusio* formed by the extensive parallels at Heb. 4:14-16 and 10:19-23 must be considered as a potentially important indicator of structural dynamics in the book. In the cohesion analysis of the previous chapter high-level cohesion shifts were identified at 4:14, 10:19, and just following 4:16. A median-level shift was also noted

---

[12] When these distinctions are marked, inversion of several of the elements may also be pointed out. First, reference to the Son as ἀρχιερεύς in 4:14-16 precedes the references to the heavenly realm and the designation Ἰησοῦν, yet, follows those elements in 10:19-23. Second, the exhortations to "hold fast" and "draw near," found in 4:14 and 4:16 respectively, are inverted in 10:22 and 10:23. Third, the reference to παρρησία finds expression at the end of 4:14-16, yet at the beginning of 10:19-23. In 4:16 the hearers are exhorted, as a final challenge of 4:14-16, to draw near (the throne of God) with confidence. In 10:19, the beginning of 10:19-23, that confidence, or assurance, to come near God is the foundational assumption of the exhortation which follows, the author stating Ἔχοντες οὖν, ἀδελφοί, παρρησίαν . . ..

as occurring shortly after 10:23 at 10:26. These shifts demonstrate that a high level of "turbulence" in the discourse surrounds both 4:14-16 and 10:19-23, which have been clearly shown to be the opening and closing of a major *inclusio*.[13]

The examination of dynamic parallels between Heb. 4:14-16 and 10:19-23 suggests that the author considered 4:14-16 to have an inherent unity. This provides one reason for extending the section begun in Heb. 3:1 all the way to 4:16, even though the elements

---

[13] Having established a breaking point between 4:13 and 4:14, Nauck also suggests the "hymn" of 4:12-13, concerning the word of God, complements the "hymn" of Heb. 1:2b-3. At least two observations are in order at this point.

First, that 4:12-13 actually constitutes "hymnic" material stands as a highly questionable proposition. So Attridge, *The Epistle to the Hebrews*, 133. Attridge points out that the passage does not evidence the poetic devices common to early Christian hymns, but rather offers "an elaborate bit of festive prose." The hymnic character of Heb. 1:2-3 has also been called into question by D. W. B. Robinson, "The Literary Structure of Hebrews 1:1-4," *Australian Journal of Biblical Archaeology* 2 (1972): 178-86, who does so on the basis of the chiastic structure of Heb. 1:1-4; and J. Frankowski, "Early Christian Hymns Recorded in the New Testament: A Reconsideration of the Question in Light of Heb 1,3," *Biblische Zeitschrift* 27 (1983): 183-94.

Yet, parts of Heb. 1:2-3 as a hymn fragment have been supported by several scholars on the bases of form and content. See, Ralph P. Martin, *Carmen Christi: Philippians ii.5-11 in recent interpretation and in the setting of early Christian worship* (Cambridge: Cambridge University Press, 1967), 18-19; Jack T. Sanders, *The New Testament Christological Hymns: Their Historical Religious Background* (Cambridge: Cambridge University Press, 1971), 92-94; Gottfried Schille, *Früchristliche Hymnen*, 2 ed. (Berlin: Evangelische Verlagsanstalt, 1965), 42; Attridge, *The Epistle to the Hebrews*, 42.

Second, the verbal parallels between 1:1-3 and 4:12-13 are limited to (1) the term θεός, also used in 1:6, 8, 9; 2:4, 9, 13, 17; 3:4, 12; 4:4, 9, 10; (2) the "powerful word" (τῷ ῥήματι τῆς δυνάμεως αὐτοῦ, 1:3) as compared with the λόγος τοῦ θεοῦ as ἐνεργής in 4:12; and (3) reference to the created order (ἐποίησεν τοὺς αἰῶνας in 1:2, κτίσις in 4:13). Also finding expression throughout 1:1-4:13, description of the "word of God" is not unique to these two passages. With reference to the created order (#3 above), Heb. 1:10 also remarks on that phenomenon.

There is, admittedly, a conceptual parallel between the notion of God "speaking" (1:1) and the statement concerning the "word of God" in 4:12-13. Yet, the concept of God speaking also finds expression throughout the intervening text (1:1-14; 2:1-4; 3:7-4:11).

It seems that the warning of Heb. 4:12-13, which speaks of the inability of anyone to escape God's piercing judgment, makes a better parallel to the warning of Heb. 2:1-4, though it does not form an *inclusio* with that passage.

The final *inclusio* noted by Wolfgang Nauck may also be labeled as questionable. The only verbal parallel between the two passages involves the opening term in each—'Αναμιμνήσκεσθε in 10:32 and Μνημονεύετε in 13:7. Nauck is correct in suggesting the passages are similar in form. Yet, they also share this similarity with 3:12-15, 6:9-12, and 12:4-17. These correspondences, found so far apart in the text, do not warrant the label *inclusio*.

parallel with 3:1 all occur in 4:14.[14] Such an extension would allow the integrity of 4:14-16 to be maintained.

If 3:1-4:16 be considered a section and 4:14-10:23 be considered a section, then an *overlap* presents itself. This dynamic cannot be ruled out as an impossibility and must be investigated further under the discussion of transitions. That a break does, in fact, occur between 4:16 and 5:1 is further supported by the next *inclusio* to be discussed.

HEB. 5:1-3 AND 7:27-28

With Heb. 5:1-3 the author begins his new section with a generalized statement concerning the *appointment* (καθίσταται) of a person to the office of high priest under the old covenant law. Although undetected by Albert Vanhoye, this statement finds echo at 7:26-28. The parallels between the two passages are displayed in fig. 17. Both passages deal with the concept of appointment to the office of high priest. The central term καθίστημι, used in 5:1 and 7:28, finds no intervening expression. Whereas Heb. 5:1-3 presents a general picture of the appointment of old covenant priests, the second embodies a comparison of those priests with the Son—the ultimate high priest appointed by God's oath. Thus, the author crafts an *inclusio* which brackets the section running from 5:1 through 7:28.

As already noted, a high-level cohesion shift occurs with Heb. 5:1, supporting the opening boundary apparently marked by the *inclusio* under consideration. A median-level cohesion shift also occurs immediately following 7:28 at Heb. 8:1. Thus, the boundaries marked by the *inclusio* at 5:1-3/ 7:26-28 correspond to cohesion shifts in the discourse of Hebrews.

HEB. 5:1 AND 5:10

The concepts of "high priest," "appointment," and "God," found in 5:1, also serve to mark the first movement within Heb. 5:1-7:28.[15] The participle form of προσαγορεύω (designate) used in 5:10 is a synonym of καθίστημι and may have been used as a substitute here

---

[14] Supra, 78.
[15] Vanhoye notes the use of ἀρχιερεύς but does not include the terms related to "appointment" or θεός as players in the inclusion. See Vanhoye, *La structure littéraire de l'Épître aux Hébreux*, 110.

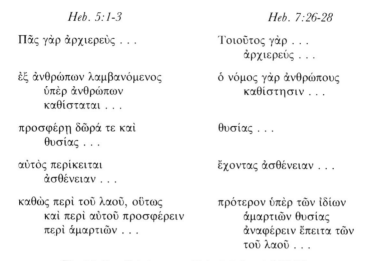

Heb. 5:1-3

Πᾶς γὰρ ἀρχιερεὺς . . .

ἐξ ἀνθρώπων λαμβανόμενος
    ὑπὲρ ἀνθρώπων
    καθίσταται . . .

προσφέρῃ δῶρά τε καὶ
    θυσίας . . .

αὐτὸς περίκειται
    ἀσθένειαν . . .

καθὼς περὶ τοῦ λαοῦ, οὕτως
    καὶ περὶ αὐτοῦ προσφέρειν
    περὶ ἁμαρτιῶν . . .

Heb. 7:26-28

Τοιοῦτος γὰρ . . .
    ἀρχιερεύς . . .

ὁ νόμος γὰρ ἀνθρώπους
    καθίστησιν . . .

θυσίας . . .

ἔχοντας ἀσθένειαν . . .

πρότερον ὑπὲρ τῶν ἰδίων
    ἁμαρτιῶν θυσίας
    ἀναφέρειν ἔπειτα τῶν
    τοῦ λαοῦ . . .

Fig. 17. Parallels between Heb. 5:1-3 and 7:26-28.

because of the central role καθίστημι plays in the *inclusio* at 5:1-3/
7:26-28. In both 5:1 and 5:10 the appointment is to the office of
ἀρχιερεύς, and in both θεός plays part in the appointment. In the
former the high priest is appointed (by the law) τὰ πρὸς τὸν θεόν,
but in the latter ὑπὸ τοῦ θεοῦ.[16]

The boundaries marked by the *inclusio* at Heb. 5:1/5:10 correspond to the high-level cohesion shifts at 5:1 and following 5:10.

Heb. 5:11 and 6:12

Beginning with Heb. 5:11 and continuing through 6:12 the author
turns to his hearers and addresses their immaturity. The phrase
νωθροὶ γεγόνατε in 5:11 is mirrored with νωθροὶ γένησθε in 6:12, in
5:11 the hearers being rebuked for laziness of hearing.[17] In 6:12 they
are encouraged to move from laziness to imitation of those who by
faith inherit the promises.

---

[16] This same contrast is clear in Heb. 7:11-28. The author makes much of Ps.
110:4 as God's own pronouncement of the Son's Melchizedekan priesthood. He
plays this over against the old covenant priesthood which came by appointment
through the law.

[17] Vanhoye, *La structure littéraire de l'Épître aux Hébreux*, 115.

Once again the head and tail boundary marked by this *inclusio* correspond to high-level cohesion shifts at those points in the discourse.

HEB. 7:1 AND 7:9-10

The statement that Melchizedek "met Abraham" stands near the beginning of the midrash on Genesis 14 found in Heb. 7:1-10. The proposition finds expression again at verses 9-10.[18] A high-level shift corresponds to the head member of the *inclusio* and a median-level shift to the tail member.

HEB. 7:11 AND 7:28

The necessity of a new priest arising according to the order of Melchizedek came about, according to the author of Hebrews, because of the imperfection of the law-ordained priesthood. These concepts of perfection (τελείωσις), priesthood (ἱερωσύνης), and law (νενομο-θέτηται) expressed in Heb. 7:11 are roughly paralleled at 7:28, a verse already noted as playing a part in the *inclusio* of 5:1-3/7:26-28. In Heb. 7:28 the law is said to appoint men who are weak to the position of high priest, but ὁ λόγος ... τῆς ὁρκωμοσίας τῆς μετὰ τὸν νόμον υἱὸν εἰς τὸν αἰῶνα τετελειωμένον.

Both the head and tail boundary of the *inclusio* correspond to median-level cohesion shifts.

HEB. 8:3 AND HEB. 10:18

At Heb. 8:3 the author repeats the generalized statement made in 5:1 concerning the appointment of a high priest under the old covenant. This time, however, the emphasis is placed on the aspect of gifts and sacrifices for sin. In 5:1 he states, Πᾶς γὰρ ἀρχιερεὺς ἐξ ἀνθρώπων λαμβανόμενος ὑπὲρ ἀνθρώπων καθίσταται τὰ πρὸς τὸν θεόν, ἵνα προσφέρῃ δῶρά τε καὶ θυσίας ὑπὲρ ἁμαρτιῶν. In Heb. 8:3 he says, πᾶς γὰρ ἀρχιερεὺς εἰς τὸ προσφέρειν δῶρά τε καὶ θυσίας καθίσταται. ὅθεν ἀναγκαῖον ἔχειν τι καὶ τοῦτον ὃ προσενέγκῃ. Notice that the statement concerning appointment precedes that concerning sacrif-

---

[18] Idem, "Literarische Struktur und theologische Botschaft des Hebräerbriefs (1. Teil)," 139.

ices in 5:1 but follows it in 8:3, the topic of sacrifice being given the more prominent role in the latter passage.

The parallel statements found at 5:1 and 8:3 do not form an *inclusio*. The *inclusio* begun in Heb. 5:1-3 has already been shown to close at 7:26-28. Rather, 5:1 and 8:3 form a special type of transition referred to in the present study as "parallel introductions." This transitional device will be dealt with later.[19]

The author's statement in 8:3 emphasizes the necessity (ἀναγκαῖον) of the heavenly High Priest having something to offer. The section which follows presents a comparison of the Son's offering with those of the earthly high priests. The concluding statement found at 10:18 wraps up the discussion, and thus closes off the *inclusio*, by way of contrast. Here, for the first time, the author states that sacrifice for sin is no longer necessary: ὅπου δὲ ἄφεσις τούτων, οὐκέτι προσφορὰ περὶ ἁμαρτίας. Thus Heb. 10:18 offers a fitting closure to the *inclusio* opened at 8:3.

HEB. 8:8-12 AND HEB. 10:15-17

Part of the quote of Jer. 31:31-34, found at Heb. 8:8-12, is repeated at 10:15-17. Since 8:7 appears to be an introduction which gives rise to the quote in 8:8-12, the head boundary of the section marked by this *inclusio* will be tentatively placed between 8:6 and 8:7. Similarly, the statement at 10:18 seems to constitute a comment on the quote just given. Therefore, the tail boundary of this *inclusio* will follow 10:18, a break shared by the inclusio of 8:3/10:18 demonstrated above.

HEB. 8:7 AND HEB. 8:13

Both Heb. 8:7 and Heb. 8:13 refer to the old covenant as displaced

Καινὴν πεπαλαίωκεν τὴν πρώτην. The word common to both passages is πρώτη, a reference to the old covenant. In 8:7 the author speaks of the new covenant as "second." Picking up on the term καινήν in the quote (8:8), he then refers to the second covenant as

---

[19] *Infra*, 104-105.

"new" in 8:13. Based on these parallel statements, Heb. 8:7 and 8:13 may be seen as forming an *inclusio*.

The head boundary marked by this *inclusio* may be tentatively placed between 8:6 and 8:7, the same head boundary noted under consideration of the *inclusio* at 8:8-12 and 10:16-17. Placed following 8:13, the tail boundary finds additional support under consideration of the next *inclusio*.

HEB. 9:1 AND Heb. 9:10

The only occurrences of the term δικαιώματα in Hebrews are found at 9:1 and 9:10. The term may be translated "regulations" and here refers to the regulations of divine worship set forth under the first covenant. The statements containing the word bracket a description of those regulations as set forth in the Torah. Since there are no intervening uses of the word and the use in Heb. 9:10 functions to provide a fitting conclusion to the immediate description of the old covenant regulations, δικαιώματα may be considered to play the key role in formation of an *inclusio* which marks a unit running from Heb. 9:1 through 9:10.[20]

HEB. 9:11-12 AND 9:28

Heb. 9:11 and 9:28 set forth a contrast between the first and the last "appearances" (παραγενόμενος in 9:11 and ὀφθήσεται in 9:28) of Christ (Χριστός). While both passages contain references to Christ's sacrificial death, the contrast lies in the purpose of the appearances. In 9:11 he came as a high priest, i.e., to take away sins. A second appearance, χωρὶς ἁμαρτίας, is the topic of 9:28. This second appearance will also be to bring deliverance to believers, a deliverance from the present age.

The embedded discourse which runs from 9:11 through 9:28 has a third reference to an "appearance" of Christ. In Heb. 9:24 the author again uses the title Χριστός and, as in 9:11, states that Christ οὐ . . . εἰς χειροποίητα εἰσῆλθεν. This reference, however, emphasizes the present role of Christ as mediator between God and believer, as the phrase νῦν ἐμφανισθῆναι suggests. Thus, the three uses of

---

[20] Vanhoye, "Literarische Struktur und theologische Botschaft des Hebräerbriefs (1. Teil)," 138.

the title Χριστός in 9:11-28 reflect a three-step, chronological progression concerning appearances of Christ:

Christ appeared to obtain redemption (9:11)	PAST
Christ now appears in God's presence (9:24)	PRESENT
Christ will appear (in relation to this creation) a second time (9:28)	FUTURE

HEB. 10:1 AND Heb. 10:14

Contrast also forms the basis for the next *inclusio* set forth in the present discussion. Analysis of these two verses reveals four sets of contrasts with which the author opened and closed the *inclusio* marking the unit running from 10:1-10:14. These contrasts are depicted in fig. 18.

Heb. 10:1	*Heb. 10:14*
ταῖς αὐταῖς θυσίαις	μιᾷ . . . προσφορᾷ
προσφέρουσιν εἰς τὸ διηνεκὲς	(τετελείωκεν) εἰς τὸ διηνεκὲς
οὐδέποτε δύναται . . . τελειῶσαι	τετελείωκεν
τοὺς προσερχομένους (under the old system)	τοὺς ἁγιαζομένους (under the new system)

Fig. 18. Contrasts in Heb. 10:1 and 10:14.

In Heb. 10:1 the author of Hebrews refers to the multiple sacrifices offered under the Law. The one sacrifice made by Jesus is the topic of Heb. 10:14. In 10:1 the sacrifices are made perpetually, while in 10:14 the perfection of the saints is perpetual. According to the former verse the Law has no ability to perfect "those who draw near" under the old system. Yet, according to the latter, Christ's one sacrifice has perfected "the ones being sanctified" under the new system.

HEB. 11:1-2 AND 11:39-40

The example list set forth in Hebrews 11 begins with the familiar Ἔστιν δὲ πίστις ἐλπιζομένων ὑπόστασις, πραγμάτων ἔλεγχος οὐ βλεπομένων. The discourse continues in 11:2 with the proposition

that by faith the elders "were spoken well of" (ἐμαρτυρήθησαν).
After building the *exempla*, providing example after example of
those who prevailed by faith, the author closes in 11:39-40 with Καὶ
οὗτοι πάντες μαρτυρηθέντες διὰ τῆς πίστεως οὐκ ἐκομίσαντο τὴν
ἐπαγγελίαν, τοῦ θεοῦ περὶ ἡμῶν κρεῖττόν τι προβλεψαμένου . . . The
terms μαρτυρηθέντες, πίστεως, and the similar προβλεψαμένου echo
terms in Heb. 11:1-2.[21]

The head boundary marked by this *inclusio* corresponds to the
high-level cohesion shift at Heb. 11:1 and the tail boundary corresponds to the median-level shift at 12:1.

SUMMARY CONCERNING INCLUSIONS IN HEBREWS

Eighteen inclusions have been identified in the present chapter.
Two primary observations may be made with reference to these uses
of *inclusio* by the author of Hebrews.

First, the head and tail members of *every inclusio* correspond to a
high or median-level cohesion shift identified in Chapter 4. This
fact suggests that corresponding shifts in "cohesion fields" can be
accurately tracked and do help in isolation of turning points in a
discourse.

Second, with the identification of inclusions in Hebrews, embedded discourse units are beginning to take shape. For example, the
great central section marked by the inclusion at 4:14-16/10:19-23
has up to four levels of embedding. Inclusions mark 5:1-7:28 and
8:3-10:18, two primary movements of the great central section.
These embedded discourses are further broken down into smaller
embedded discourse units: 5:1-10, 5:11-6:12, 7:1-10, 7:11-28, and
8:8-10:17. The unit running from 8:8 to 10:17 may be broken down
further: 8:7-13, 9:1-10, 9:11-28, and 10:1-14.

Furthermore, the elements forming inclusions are often stacked
side-by-side with elements forming inclusions which mark the next
level of discourse embedding. The front member of the inclusion
opening 5:1-7:28 (5:1-3) immediately follows Heb. 4:14-16, the
front member of the inclusion marking the great central section.

---

[21] Vanhoye notes the function of the forms of μαρτυρέω and πίστις in 11:1-2 and
11:39 as constituting an *inclusio* but takes βλεπόμενων of 11:1 to form an *inclusio* with
the use of the same form in 11:7. See Vanhoye, *La structure littéraire de l'Épître aux
Hébreux*, 294.

The closing of the inclusion marking 5:1-7:28 (7:26-28) is followed by the opening of 8:3-10:18 just three verses later. Note that four inclusions, marking different levels of embedded discourses, are closed *in succession* from Heb. 10:14 through 10:23. The *inclusio* marking 10:1-14 is closed at 10:14, the one marking 8:8-10:17 at 10:15-17, the one marking 8:3-10:18 at 10:18, and the inclusion marking 4:14-10:23 at 10:19-23.

Chapters 4 and 5 serve two primary purposes in laying a foundation for the rest of the study. First, these chapters provide means by which units in the discourse may be isolated. If just unit boundaries marked by high-level cohesion shifts[22] and those marked by a head or tail member of an inclusion are taken into consideration, the discourse units thus far isolated are 1:1-4, 1:5-14, 2:1-4, 2:5-9, 2:10-18, 3:1-6, 3:7-11, 3:12-19, 4:1-2, 4:3-11, 4:12-13, 4:14-16, 5:1-10, 5:11-6:3, 6:4-8, 6:9-12, 6:13-20, 7:1-10, 7:11-28, 8:1-2, 8:3-6, 8:7-13, 9:1-10, 9:11-28, 10:1-14, 10:15-18, 10:19-25, 10:26-39, 11:1-40, 12:1-2, 12:3-17, 12:18-29, 13:1-19, 13:20-21, and 13:22-25.

Second, Chapter 5 also offers a point of departure for discussion of the interrelationship of those units isolated thus far. The study now turns to consider the role lexical items play in building cohesion between discourse units in Hebrews.

---

[22] At this point of the study the jury is still out on the value of all median-level shifts. Further consideration of the role of the median-level shifts not confirmed by a member of an inclusion will take place later in the volume.

CHAPTER SIX

LEXICAL COHESION BETWEEN TWO
OR MORE DISCOURSE UNITS
IN HEBREWS

An author has several means by which he may indicate relationships between the individual units which make up his discourse. Inclusions have already been shown to play a part in the "grouping" of embedded discourse units. Two other means by which the joint venture of two or more discourse units may be demonstrated are (1) identification of lexical or pronominal items used throughout a section, and (2) identification of specific transition techniques used by the author.

LEXICAL AND PRONOMINAL COHESION IN HEBREWS

Elements Found throughout the Discourse

Text-linguistic analysis seeks in part to uncover semantic threads which relate sections of a discourse. Semantic threads in a discourse most often are woven with the same, or related, lexical items. Such items may be used repeatedly in two or more units, enhancing the semantic relationship between those units.[1]

---

[1] Albert Vanhoye, following A. Descamps, set forth "characteristic terms" as one means of discerning the structure of Hebrews. Vanhoye, *La structure littéraire de l'Épître aux Hébreux*, 37-46; Descamps, "La structure de l'Épître aux Hébreux," 254-57, 333-37.

As pointed out in Chapter 3, Vanhoye's concept of "characteristic terms" roughly corresponds to the designation "lexical cohesion." Lexical elements may play a unifying role in individual units of a discourse, but also may span several units, indicating a relationship between those units.

The same lexical item may be used either by reiteration, the repeating of the same item with the same referent, or collocation, the repeating of the same item without the same referent. See supra, 52-53.

Related, though not identical, elements may be categorized as follows: (1) those based on similarity, including (a) overlapping relations (proper synonymy), (b) contiguous relations (improper synonymy), and (c) inclusive relations (hyponymy); and (2) those based on oppositeness, including (a) binary relations (antonymy), and (b) multiple relations (incompatibility). See Silva, *Biblical Words and Their Meaning: An Introduction to Lexical Semantics*, 119-36.

Scholars have pointed to several concepts around which the book of Hebrews may be understood to cohere, including "covenant," "promise," and "the exaltation."[2] However, the most important items used in building lexical and pronominal cohesion in the whole of Hebrews are (1) the term θεός, along with pronominal references to God, (2) designations and pronominal items used with reference to God's Son, Jesus, (3) terms semantically related to the concept "the word of God," and (4) pronominal references to members of the Christian community, used either of the author of the book himself, his hearers, or both.[3]

The term θεός occurs sixty-eight times in the book, being found in thirty of the thirty-five units previously isolated in this study.[4] This frequently reiterated lexical item is flanked by numerous pronominal references to God throughout the work. Thus from the opening thought to the benediction, "God" remains a governing concept in the discourse.

Second, various designations are used to refer to Jesus throughout Hebrews, including υἱός, πρωτότοκος, θεός, Ἰησοῦς, ἀρχιερεύς, Κύριος, Χριστός, Ἰησοῦς Χριστός, and ποιμένα. These designations, along with pronominals having Jesus as the referent, may also be found in thirty of the thirty-five units of the book.[5] Throughout the discourse the author keeps his hearers focused on the One first introduced in the book as υἱῷ (1:2).

A third concept introduced in the first statement of the discourse is "the word of God." Through use of the verbs λέγω, εἶπον, and λαλέω, as well as the terms λόγος, ῥῆμα, and φωνή the hearers are continually confronted with God's spoken word, most often ad-

---

[2] For a summary of various theological approaches to understanding the organization of Hebrews see Übelacker, *Der Hebräerbrief als Appell*, 47.

[3] Other important terms spread throughout the discourse are those related to *"heaven"* (οὐρανός: Heb. 1:10, 4:14, 7:26, 8:1, 9:23-24, 11:12, 12:23-26; ἐπουράνιος: Heb. 3:1, 6:4, 8:5, 9:23, 11:16, 12:22); *"inheritance"* (κληρονομέω: Heb. 1:4,14, 6:12, 12:17; κληρονομία: Heb. 9:15, 11:8; κληρονόμος: Heb. 1:2, 6:17, 11:7); *"better"* (κρείττων: Heb. 1:4, 6:9, 7:7,19,22, 8:6, 9:23, 10:34, 11:16,35,40, 12:24); *"perfect"* (τέλειος: Heb. 5:14, 9:11; τελειότης: Heb. 6:1; τελειόω: Heb. 2:10, 5:9, 7:19,28, 9:9, 10:1,14, 11:40, 12:23; τελείωσις: Heb. 7:11; τελειωτής: Heb. 12:2); and *"sin,"* forms of ἁμαρτία being found twenty-five times throughout the discourse.

[4] The exceptions are 8:1-2; 8:3-6; 9:1-10; 10:15-18; and 13:22-25. However, God is referred to as τῆς μεγαλωσύνης in Heb. 8:1 and implied in 8:3-6. The Holy Spirit is referred to in 10:15-18.

[5] The exceptions are Heb. 4:3-11; 6:9-12; 8:7-13; 9:1-10; 10:15-18.

dressed to the Son or presented as directly applicable to the hearers themselves.[6]

Finally, constant pronominal references to the speaker, or the hearers, or the community as a whole, permeate the book of Hebrews, especially the hortatory sections. Again found in the opening statement of the discourse, references to the speaker, his hearers, or both occur in twenty-nine of the thirty-five previously identified units of the discourse.[7]

Additional Elements Providing Lexical Cohesion in Subsections of Hebrews

The elements detailed before as providing cohesion throughout the macro-discourse also provide cohesion to subsections of the book of Hebrews. Other terms, however, join these elements in building lexical cohesion in smaller sections of the book.

For example, the term υἱός, used both of Jesus and believers in Jesus, builds lexical cohesion between all but two of the units in Heb. 1:1-5:10.[8] When this section is broken down, several subsections cohere around certain lexical items. The term ἄγγελος further provides lexical cohesion to 1:1-2:18. A variety of terms related to exalted status pepper 1:5-14.[9] The concept of "subjection" gives cohesion to 2:5-9, and references to family relationships along with references to suffering bond 2:10-18.[10]

Terms related to "faith" and "faithfulness" enhance the cohesion of 3:1-4:13. References to Moses aid in the bonding of 3:1-6 and the terms σήμερον and κατάπαυσις are the most important items in 3:7-4:11.

The terms ἀρχιερεύς and ἱερεύς aid in bonding the units found

---

[6] Forms of λέγω, occurring thirty-two times in Hebrews, are the author's favorite introductory formulae. This pattern stands in line with that of a Jewish-hellenistic homily. See Thyen, *Der Stil des jüdisch-hellenistischen Homilie*, 69-74; McCullough, "The Old Testament Quotations in Hebrews," 363-79. Forms of λαλέω are found sixteen times, forms of εἶπον six times, forms of λόγος twelve times, ῥῆμα four, and φωνή five.

[7] The exceptions are 1:5-14; 5:1-10; 6:4-8; 8:3-6; 8:7-13; and 9:1-10.

[8] The two exceptions are 3:7-4:2 and 4:3-13.

[9] E.g., πρωτότοκον (1:6), θρόνος (1:8), ῥάβδος (1:8), βασιλείας (1:8), παρὰ τοὺς μετόχους (1:9), οὐρανοί (1:10), δεξιῶν (1:13).

[10] Supra, 63-65.

from 4:14 through 10:25.[11] This broad section may be divided into 5:1-7:28 and 8:1-10:18. In the former, the name Μελχισέδεκ and terms related to appointment may be added to the list of cohesive lexical items.[12] The lexical item διαθήκη and those semantically clustered around the concept of "offering" add to the lexical cohesion of 8:1-10:18.[13] Cohesion builds with references to Abraham in 6:13-7:10 and with references to "perfection," the Law, and the concept of eternality ("forever") in 7:11-28.

The theme of "endurance," woven throughout the units found in 10:32-12:17, characterizes that section of the discourse.[14] In Heb. 10:32-12:3 lexical cohesion rises dramatically via the term πίστις, which the author utilizes twenty-seven times in that portion of the book. Finally, the terms πῦρ and οὐρανός lexically join the two units at 12:18-29.

Conclusion

The present discussion of lexical and pronominal cohesion in Hebrews demonstrates that lexical items and pronouns function to effect semantic relationships between groups of discourse units. As with the inclusions identified in Hebrews, these relationships are shown to be hierarchical.[15] Smaller groups of units, while benefitting from words used to lexically bond larger blocks of the discourse, utilize their own lexical material to provide semantic distinctiveness from other groups of units on the same level of the discourse. Fig. 19 depicts this dynamic.

For example, while both 5:1-7:28 and 8:1-10:18 benefit from those lexical items which offer cohesion in the broader discourse (i.e., "priest," "high priest," "God," references to God, references to Jesus, etc.), they also find distinction from one another through

---

[11] Ἱερεύς occurs thirteen times and ἀρχιερεύς fifteen times in 4:14-10:25. Only three occurrences of the latter term and one of the former are found outside this block. However, the terms are not found in the hortatory units at 5:11-6:12.

[12] Speaking of "appointment" the author uses the term καθίστημι in 5:1 and 7:28; καλούμενος in 5:4; forms of γίνομαι in 5:5, 5:9, 6:20, 7:16, and 7:22; προσαγορευθείς in 5:10; and λέγεσθαι in 7:11.

[13] E.g., the verb προσφέρω occurs fourteen times from 8:3-10:12 and θύσια finds expression thirteen times.

[14] The verb ὑπομένω is found at Heb. 10:32, 12:2, 12:3, and 12:7, which ὑπομονή occurs at Heb. 10:36 and 12:1.

[15] Supra, 88-89.

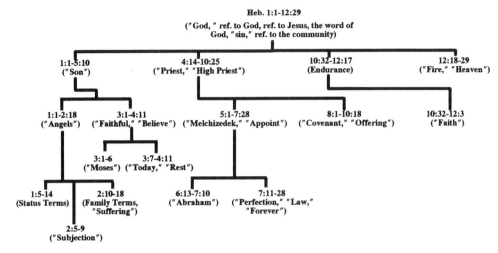

Fig. 19. Examples of elements in Hebrews which build lexical and pronominal cohesion at different levels of the discourse.

the name "Melchizedek" and the concept of appointment (5:1-7:28) as well as the term διαθήκη and terms related to "offering" (8:1-10:18).

The hierarchical relationships between units in Hebrews, disclosed in the analysis of lexical and pronominal cohesion, roughly correspond to those highlighted in the discussion of inclusions in Chapter 5. Lexical and pronominal analysis has further shown that the units from Heb. 1:1-5:10 relate around the concept of υἱός and those from 10:32-12:17 cohere via the concept of "endurance."

This brief analysis of lexical and pronominal cohesion, however, has raised problems at a number of points where lexical items seem to suggest an overlap between sections of the discourse. For example, the use of the term υἱός in 5:1-10 would suggest an association of that passage especially with 1:1-3:6. However, the terms Μελχισέδεκ and καθίστημι, give cohesion to 5:1-7:28. Numerous cases of this phenomenon occur in Hebrews, which brings this study to the question of transitions.

TRANSITIONS IN THE STRUCTURE OF *HEBREWS*

One of the most neglected topics in discussions on the structure of Hebrews is the author's use of various transitional techniques.

Transitions effect a special type of lexical cohesion in a discourse. Through transitions an author executes smooth passage from one unit to the next, utilizing important lexical items strategically placed at the beginning or end of a text unit.

The author of Hebrews was a master at executing effective transitions from one segment of his discourse to the next. His methods must be analyzed in order to discern objectively which elements of the discourse are transitional and what type of transitions are carried out by those elements.

The suggestions which follow are based partly on an article by H. Van Dyke Parunak entitled "Transitional Techniques in the Bible."[16] Parunack deals with "The Keyword," "The Link," three varieties of "The Linked Keyword," and two types of "The Hinge," clearly demonstrating the use of each in the Bible.[17]

In the present study these techniques are given different designations, and three other techniques discerned in Hebrews are added: "Distant Hook Words," "Overlapping Constituents," and "Parallel Introductions." Hebrews also presents two variations on Parunack's "The Hinge" transition. These variations, in this study designated "The Woven Intermediary Transition" and "The Ingressive Intermediary Transition," are discussed.

All of the transition techniques are grouped under one of two broad categories. "Constituent Transitions" are those in which the transitional element is located in one or more of the constituents (always an introduction or conclusion) of the two units of material being joined together by the transition. "Intermediary Transitions"

---

[16] H. Van Dyke Parunak, "Transitional Techniques in the Bible," *Journal of Biblical Literature* 102 (1983): 525-48. Also, on the use of transitions in discourse see Berger, *Exegese des Neuen Testaments*, 13-27; Neeley, "A Discourse Analysis of Hebrews," 8-10; Eugene A. Nida and Charles R. Taber, *The Theory and Practice of Translation*, Helps for Translators (Leiden: E. J. Brill, 1969), 137-46.

In ancient Greek rhetoric the *transitio* was a figure which "'. . . briefly recalls what has been said, and likewise briefly sets forth what is to follow next . . .'" See Watson, *Invention, Arrangement, and Style*, 202.

[17] Parunak's first category, "The Keyword," is omitted in the present discussion since it has more to do with the cohesion of two segments of material than with transition between the two. Parunack admits this stating, "In one sense, we belittle the keyword technique in classing it as a transitional tool. It is a far more general phenomenon." See Parunack, "Transitional Techniques in the Bible," 530. What Parunak calls "the keyword technique" corresponds to the use of general lexical cohesion dealt with supra, 90-93.

are those effected by an intermediary unit of text which stands between two major sections of the discourse. The unit used to make an intermediary transition belongs neither exclusively to the discourse unit which precedes it nor the one which follows, but contains elements of both.

Constituent Transitions

Hook Words[18]
What Parunack calls "The Link" has already been discussed with reference to the literary device designated *mot-crochet* by Leon Vaganay.[19] By use of a common word at the end of one section and at the beginning of the next the author generated a transition between the two sections. The relationship may be depicted as in fig. 20.

For example, in Heb. 2:17 at the conclusion of the section on the Son having become lower than the angels to suffer and identify with man (2:10-18), Jesus is first called ἀρχιερεύς. In Heb. 3:1 the author begins a new section of material, turning to address his hearers directly. In Heb. 3:1 Jesus is again referred to as "high priest" (ἀρχιερέα). These are the only two occurrences of the word in chapters two and three. The use of this hookword at the end of one section and the beginning of the next makes a smooth transition between the two.

Distant Hook Words
Hebrews seems to present an ingenious variation on the hook word technique by which the author "joins" units of the same genre,

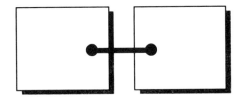

Fig. 20. Hook words used as a transition device.

---

[18] The designation "hook word" is used in this study rather than Parunack's designation "link" since the former term has been utilized extensively in the present debate.
[19] Supra, 12.

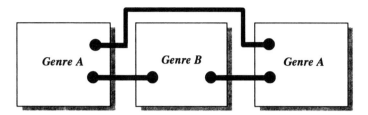

Fig. 21. Distant hook words used as a transition device.

though those units are separated by an intervening unit of a different genre. Where a unit of genre A is followed by a unit of genre B, which is in turn followed by another unit of genre A, the author uses at least two sets of hook words—one to attach the first unit of genre A to the unit of genre B and another to attach the first unit of genre A to the next unit of genre A in the discourse. Fig. 21 presents a graphic depiction of this pattern.

Joining the Expositional Blocks

At three points in Hebrews expositional material precedes a hortatory block, which in turn is followed by a resumption of exposition. This occurs at 1:14/2:1-4/2:5, 2:18/3:1-4:16/5:1, and 5:10/5:11-6:20/ 7:1.

First, 1:5-14 stands tied to 2:1-4 by the hook word σωτηρία (1:14, 2:3). Heb. 2:1-4, on the other hand, links with 2:5-9 via the hook word λαλέω (2:3, 2:5) and the forms of μαρτυρέω (2:4, 2:6). Thus far, these links fall into the pattern for hook words as described.

However, the exposition in 1:5-14 may also be seen as tied to 2:5-9, the next expository section. Forms of the word μέλλω (1:14, 2:5) and the use, once again, of ἄγγελος (1:13, 2:5) connect the two expository blocks. In 2:5 the author returns to the exposition comparing the Son with the angels, a topic from which he had briefly departed following 1:14.[20]

Second, five terms and phrases found in Heb. 2:17-18 also occur

[20] There is a very real sense in which 2:1-4 must not be disconnected from 1:1-14. As will be demonstrated below, 2:1-4 presents a rhetorical climax which flows from 1:1-14. The point made here remains, however, that 2:5 resumes the discussion of the Son vis-à-vis the angels. Heb. 2:1-4 offers an implication of the comparison made in 1:1-14, while 2:5-9 provides a continuation of the comparison.

at 5:1-3. These are the phrases τὰ πρὸς τὸν θεόν (2:17, 5:1) and τοῦ λαοῦ (2:17, 5:3), along with the words ἁμαρτία (2:17; 5:1,3), ὀφείλω (2:17, 5:3), and ἀρχιερεύς (2:17, 5:1). Thus, the expository block which ends at 2:18 is tied to the initial statement of the next expository unit (5:1-10).

There is a third, final place in Hebrews where exposition is followed by exhortation, followed in turn by exposition. At Heb. 5:11 a hortatory digression interrupts the exposition begun in 5:1. That exposition resumes at 7:1. References to Melchizedek provide the hook words and the distant hook words which join 5:1-10 to the hortatory section which follows (5:11-6:20), that hortatory section to the following expository section (7:1-28), and the initial exposition in 5:1-10 to the exposition resumed in 7:1.

In Heb. 5:10, the last verse before the hortatory digression, the author states . . . προσαγορευθεὶς ὑπὸ τοῦ θεοῦ ἀρχιερεὺς κατὰ τὴν τάξιν Μελχισέδεκ. The first phrase of the hortatory unit reads, Περὶ οὗ πολὺς ἡμῖν ὁ λόγος. The pronoun οὗ, which refers to Melchizedek (i.e., "with reference to whom"), serves as the hook word, tying the hortatory section to the preceeding exposition. At the end of the hortatory unit the repetition of Μελχισέδεκ in 6:20 and 7:1 "hooks" the hortatory block with the exposition of 7:1-28. The reference in 7:1 also performs the duty of a distant hook word, linking 7:1-28 back to 5:1-10.

Thus, in every instance in Hebrews where hortatory material follows exposition and in turn is followed by exposition, the author not only uses hook words to tie the blocks together, as Vaganay and Vanhoye have suggested, but he also uses what may be designated "distant hook words" to "jump" the hortatory section and resume his exposition.

A noteworthy variation to this exposition-exhortation- exposition pattern involves the relationship between 2:17-18 and 4:14-16, a unit already shown to be the head member of a prominent *inclusio* marking a large, mostly expositional, portion of Hebrews.[21]

Use of the distant hook words ἀρχιερεύς (2:17, 5:1) and ἁμαρτία (2:17; 5:1,3) have already been noted. These two terms, along with three other concepts, also function to connect the end of 2:10-18 to 4:14-16. The five distant hook words used to tie these two passages together are "high priest" (ἀρχιερεύς in 2:17; ἀρχιερέα in 4:14 and

---

[21] Supra, 79-82.

4:15), "sin" (ἁμαρτίας in 2:17 and 4:15), "merciful" and "mercy" (ἐλεήμων in 2:17; ἔλεος in 4:16), "tempted" (πειρασθείς and πειρα-ζομένοις in 2:18; πεπειρασμένον in 4:15), and "help" (βοηθῆσαι in 2:18; βοήθειαν in 4:16).[22] Thus, the correspondences between Heb. 2:17-18 and 4:14-16 produce a strong transition between 2:10-18 and 4:14-16.[23] This phenomenon intimates the uniqueness of Heb. 4:14-16 in the development of the discourse.

Joining the Hortatory Blocks

The author not only links his expository sections in the fashion described above, but he also joins the hortatory blocks in like manner. If Heb. 4:14-16, a unit which seems to be specially related to expositional material, is bracketed, the exhortation-exposition-exhortation pattern may be found at 2:4/2:5-18/3:1, 4:13/4:14-5:10/5:11, and 6:20/7:1-10:18/10:19.

At the end of 2:1-4, the first hortatory unit in the discourse, one reads καὶ πνεύματος ἁγίου μερισμοῖς κατὰ τὴν αὐτοῦ θέλησιν. The term ἁγίου also finds expression at 3:1, the very beginning of the next hortatory unit: Ὅθεν, ἀδελφοί ἅγιοι . . . There may also be a

---

[22] Heb. 2:17-18 and 4:14-16 are the only two passages in the book in which forms of ἐλεόω are found. The only other occurrence of a form of βοηθέω appears in the quote at Heb. 13:6 (Κύριος ἐμοὶ βοηθός). Forms of πειράζω occur elsewhere only in the quote at 3:9 and the references to Old Testament figures in 11:17 and 11:37. The only use of ἀρχιερεύς between these two passages is that already noted in 3:1 and the only intervening use of ἁμαρτία is found in 3:13.

[23] As noted in Chapter 1 (supra, 11-17), Leon Vaganay and Albert Vanhoye both followed F. Thien's suggestion that ἐλεήμων . . . καὶ πιστὸς ἀρχιερεύς was an inverted announcement to two themes. They understood 3:1-4:13 (Vaganay extended this section to 4:16 and Vanhoye to 4:14) to deal with Jesus as "faithful" and 4:14-5:10 to deal with Jesus as "merciful" (or "compassionate"). The "faithfulness of the Son" is only dealt with in 3:1-6 as an introduction to the broader exhortation for the hearers to be faithful (3:7-4:13). Heb. 4:14-5:10 (or 5:1-10 for Vaganay) does not primarily deal with Jesus as "compassionate" or "merciful" but serves as an introduction to 5:1-7:28 on the appointment of the Son as high priest. The priest who can deal gently with the ignorant, spoken of in Heb. 5:2, is not even a reference to the Son, as the parallel with that verse, found in 7:27-28, demonstrates.

It may be that Thien, Vaganay, Vanhoye, and followers misunderstood the function of the author's use of ἔλεος in 4:16. It was not meant to serve as the key word announcing the author's theme in 5:1-10. Rather, it was one of several terms used to "hook" the earlier expository section on the Son's temporary local inferiority to the angels to the great central section on the appointment and heavenly offering of the superior high priest.

play on words between μερισμοῖς ("distributions") of 2:4 and μέτοχοι ("partakers")of 3:1.

Second, at the end of 4:13 the reader is confronted with the highly stylized construction ἡμῖν ὁ λόγος, a phrase which is repeated in the opening statement of the next hortatory block (5:11): Περὶ οὗ πολὺς ἡμῖν ὁ λόγος . . .

Third, at the end of the hortatory section running from 5:11-6:20, in Heb. 6:19-20 the author proclaims that Jesus (Ἰησοῦς), the forerunner (πρόδρομος), has entered (εἰσῆλθεν) within the curtain (εἰς τὸ ἐσώτερον τοῦ καταπετάσματος) "on our behalf" (ὑπὲρ ἡμῶν). At 10:19-20, the opening statement of the next hortatory section, the author suggests the believer now has *confidence* to pass through the entrance (εἰς τὴν εἴσοδον) of the Holy Place by the blood of Jesus (Ἰησοῦ), by a new way which he opened (ἐνεκαίνισεν) "for us" (ἡμῖν) through the curtain (διὰ τοῦ καταπετάσματος), which the author identifies with Jesus' flesh.

Conclusion Concerning Distant Hook Words
A transition device, labeled "Distant Hook Words" in the present study, has been shown to effect the joining of units of the same genre which are structurally separated by an intervening unit of a different genre. The one anomaly in Hebrews seems to be Heb. 4:14-16, a hortatory passage which is clearly linked to Heb. 2:17-18, an expositional passage. That the author used distant hook words to link units of the same genre, separated by an intervening unit of a different genre, would suggest an interrelationship between those sections of the book which share a common genre. This hypothesis must be further tested in constituent analysis of the macro-discourse.

Hooked Key Words
The designation "hooked key words" refers to a transition being effected either by (1) a characteristic term used in the second unit and introduced in the conclusion of the first unit, (2) a characteristic term in the first unit used in the introduction of the next, or (3) a combination of the two. All three patterns are graphically depicted in fig. 22.

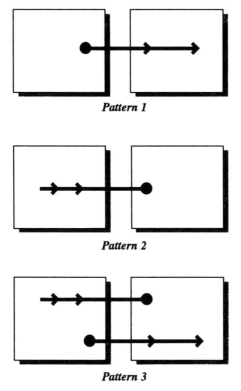

Fig. 22. Patterns of hooked key words.

Heb. 1:4 presents a clear example of pattern # 1.[24] In verse 4 the author states τοσούτῳ κρείττων γενόμενος τῶν ἀγγέλων ὅσῳ διαφορώτερον παρ' αὐτοὺς κεκληρονόμηκεν ὄνομα. This verse is both semantically and syntactically tied to the exaltation statement in 1:3. The term γενόμενος in verse four is a temporal participle which refers to the finite verb ἐκάθισεν. Thus, structurally verse 4 belongs to Heb. 1:1-4.

---

[24] Parunack, "Transitional Techniques in the Bible," 536. Leon Vaganay lists the following example as a *mot-crochet* and Vanhoye presents it as a combination of *mot-crochet* with "announcement of a theme." See Vaganay, "Le Plan de L'Épître aux Hébreux," 271-72; Vanhoye, *La structure littéraire de l'Épître aux Hébreux*, 54-57.

Five other examples of this pattern are found in the author's use of ἀρχιερέα in 4:14-16 and throughout the great central section of the book; Μελχισέδεκ at 6:20 and throughout chapter seven; οὐρανῶν at 7:26 and throughout 8:1-10:18; διαθήκης in 7:22 and throughout 8:6-10:18; and in the use of πίστις in 10:39 and throughout chapter eleven.

The semantic content of verse 4, however, also points ahead to the main theme of the next section on the Son's superiority to the angels. The term ἄγγελος stands as a characteristic term, or "key word" for 1:5-2:18, being used ten times in that section and only twice thereafter. Thus, in the final statement of the exordium (1:1-4) the author introduces the topic of his next section and produces a transition between the two blocks of material.

A possible use of pattern #2, in which a characteristic term in the first unit is used at the beginning of the following unit, may be seen in the author's use of ἄγγελος in Heb. 2:2. The author hooks Heb. 2:1-4 to 1:5-14 by the hook word σωτηρία (1:14, 2:3). The term ἄγγελος, a key word for 1:5-14 also used in 2:2, aids the connection between the two sections.

The seam between Heb. 2:5-9 and 2:10-18 presents a special challenge to the analyst. This challenge, in part, results from the type of transition used at this point in the discourse. Here the author uses a transition device along the lines of pattern #3, in which a characteristic term in the first block finds expression in the introduction of the second block and a characteristic term from the second block is utilized in the conclusion of the first. The key word δόξῃ, used in 2:5-9 at 2:7 and 2:9, also appears in the introduction to 2:10-18, where the author states, Ἔπρεπεν γάρ αὐτῷ, δι' ὅν τὰ πάντα καὶ δι' οὗ τὰ πάντα, πολλοὺς υἱοὺς εἰξ δόξαν ἀγαγόντα. Two key words from 2:10-18 are used in the conclusion of 2:5-9. These are πάθημα and θάνατος, which play major roles in communication of the main topic of 2:10-18, i.e., the Son became lower than the angels to identify with man, suffer, and die. The former is used in 2:10 and 2:18, aiding the formation of the *inclusio*. The latter finds expression in 2:14 and 2:15.

Overlapping Constituents
The designation "Overlapping Constituents" refers to a passage used simultaneously as the conclusion of one block of material and the introduction to the next. In this pattern the conclusion of section A equals the introduction of section B, as depicted in fig. 23.

The two occurrences of overlapping constituents in Hebrews are found at 4:14-16 and 10:19-25, passages which also form the *inclusio* around the second major movement of the author's expository material. Heb. 4:14-16 constitutes the conclusion to 3:1-4:16, the references to "Jesus" as "high priest" and to the believers' "confession"

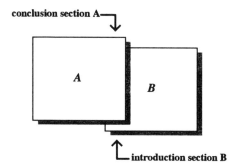

Fig. 23. Overlapping constituents as a transition device.

(4:14-15) forming the close of an *inclusio* opened in 3:1. Heb. 4:14-16 is unified with 3:1-4:13 in genre, playing a part in exhorting the hearers to take specific actions.

Yet, 4:14-16 plays a crucial role in the exposition found in 5:1-10:18, containing the opening of an important *inclusio* by which that great block of material is marked. With the reference to Jesus as a "high priest" who has passed "through the heavens," 4:14-16 is linked conceptually with the two main movements of 5:1-10:18 concerning the Son's appointment as high priest (5:1-7:28) and his superior offering in heaven (8:3-10:18). Therefore, 4:14-16 constitutes the conclusion for one section and the introduction for the next.

Heb. 10:19-25, on the other hand, closes the *inclusio* which the author opened at 4:14-16. Yet it also serves as an effective introduction to the hortatory material which follows. Conceptually, 10:19-25 is linked with the great central section on Christ's appointment as high priest, His offering "within the veil," and the believer's cleansing from sin. The primary hooked key words here are ἁγίων (see especially Hebrews 9), αἵματι, and ἱερέα μέγαν.

Nevertheless, as the first hortatory discourse the author has taken up since 6:20, 10:19-25 stands as a fitting introduction to the rest of the book. Beginning at 10:19 and continuing through the conclusion the author's aim is to spur his hearers to action based on the truths he has expounded thus far. Heb. 10:19-25, therefore, is conceptually both the conclusion to 4:14-10:18 as well as the hortatory introduction to the rest of the book.[25]

Parallel Introductions
One final type of constituent transition used in Hebrews must be mentioned. "Parallel Introductions," depicted in fig. 24, refers to the use of roughly parallel statements at the beginnings of two successive discourse units. As has been noted in the discussion on use of *inclusio* in Hebrews, this phenomenon occurs in 5:1 and 8:3.[26] In 5:1 the author states, Πᾶς γὰρ ἀρχιερεὺς ἐξ ἀνθρώπων λαμβανόμενος ὑπὲρ ἀνθρώπων καθίσταται τὰ πρὸς τὸν θεόν, ἵνα προσφέρῃ δῶρά τε καὶ θυσίας ὑπὲρ ἁμαρτιῶν. Heb. 8:3 roughly repeats this statement: πᾶς γὰρ ἀρχιερεὺς εἰς τὸ προσφέρειν δῶρά τε καὶ θυσίας καθίσταται.

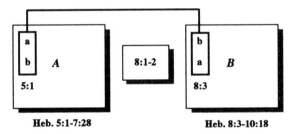

Heb. 5:1-7:28   **Heb. 8:3-10:18**

Fig. 24. Parallel introductions used in Heb. 5:1 and 8:3 as a transitional tool.

The two parts of this repeated proposition contain the two main topics of 4:14-10:25. The appointment of the Son is expounded in 5:1-7:28, and the superior offering of the appointed high priest is explicated in 8:3-10:18. Notice that in Heb. 5:1, the introduction to the discourse unit on "appointment," καθίσταται precedes the statement concerning "gifts and offerings." In Heb. 8:3, the introduc-

[25] This provides an explanation for why scholars such as Donald Guthrie, F. F. Bruce, and R. C. H. Lenski end the central section at 10:18 while others such as Harold Attridge and Wolfgang Nauck extend it to include 10:19 and following. See Guthrie, *Introduction to the New Testament*, 728-33; Bruce, *The Epistle to the Hebrews*, vii-x; Lenski, *The Interpretation of the Epistle to the Hebrews and the Epistle of James*, 27; Attridge, *The Epistle to the Hebrews*, 18-19; Nauck, "Zum Aufbau des Hebräerbriefs," 203.
[26] Supra, 84-85.

tion to the section on "the superior offering," προσφέρειν δῶρά τε καὶ θυσίας precedes καθίσταται.

Another use of parallel introductions is found in the quote of Ps. 2:7 at Heb. 1:5 and then at Heb. 5:5. The first of these quotations opens the movement of the author's discourse dealing with the position of the Son in relation to the angels (1:5-2:18). The term υἱός in the quote is a characteristic term all the way from 1:1 through 5:8, finding expression ten times.

Heb. 5:1-10 constitutes the introduction to 5:1-7:28, which deals with the appointment of the Son as high priest. In this introduction the author repeats his quote of Ps. 2:7 and then, by virtue of *gezerah shawah* joins it to Ps. 110:4, the pronoun σύ providing the verbal analogy. God, who made an oath, or proclamation, concerning Jesus as "Son" (the main designation for Jesus in 1:1-2:18), also made an oath, or proclamation, concerning Jesus as a priest according to the order of Melchizedek (the main designation for Jesus in 5:1-7:28). Thus, the repeating of Ps. 2:7 opens the way for a discussion of the proclamation found in Ps. 110:4. This plays a part in effecting a transition from the first section on Christ as Son (1:1-2:18 primarily) to the section on Christ as high priest (5:1-10:18).

Intermediary Transitions

Intermediary transitions are those carried out by a unit of text which stands between two major sections of the discourse. Parunack refers to this transition technique as "The Hinge" and identifies two subcategories of the technique. These are the "Direct Hinge," which we designate "The Direct Intermediary Transition," and the "Inverted Hinge," labeled here as "The Inverted Intermediary Transition."

A direct intermediary transition is one in which the intermediary unit of text first contains an element of the preceding discourse and then introduces an element prominent in the discourse which follows. The second type of intermediary transition, the inverted intermediary transition, contains elements of the preceding discourse unit at the end of the transitional unit and elements of the following discourse unit at the beginning of the transitional unit. Therefore, the main concepts effecting the transition are "inverted" in order in the transitional unit. No expression of this pattern seems to exist in Hebrews.

Two variations on this pattern, however, are detected in Hebrews. The first may be labeled "The Woven Intermediary Transition." In this pattern characteristic elements of the preceding discourse unit and the following discourse unit are intertwined in the transitional unit. The second may be labeled the "Ingressive Intermediary Transition." In this pattern the author makes an abrupt digression from a topic under discussion. Immediately following the main body of the digression he crafts an intermediary unit; this utilizes terms from the digression and terms serving to lead into a resumption of the topic discussed before the digression.

Graphical depictions of all four patterns of intermediary transitions are found in fig. 25.

The Direct Intermediary Transition

Heb. 8:1-2 provides an example of the direct intermediary transition. It will be argued on several bases that the great central section of Hebrews has two movements. The first, 5:1-7:28, deals with the appointment of the Son as high priest. The second, 8:3-10:18, describes the heavenly (and thus superior) offering of the appointed high priest.

Heb. 8:1-2 stands between these two blocks of material. The author first states, Κεφάλαιον δὲ ἐπὶ τοῖς λεγομένοις, τοιοῦτον ἔχομεν ἀρχιερέα, ὃς ἐκάθισεν ἐν δεξιᾷ τοῦ θρόνου τῆς μεγαλωσύνης, clearly referring to what he has covered thus far. He continues, however, ἐν τοῖς οὐρανοῖς, τῶν ἁγίων λειτουργὸς καὶ τῆς σκηνῆς τῆς ἀληθινῆς, ἣν ἔπηξεν ὁ κύριος, οὐκ ἄνθρωπος. The reference to ἐν τοῖς οὐρανοῖς presents a change to the author's allusion to Ps. 110:1 in Heb. 1:3 as well as the quote of Ps. 110:1 in Heb. 1:13. This addition, in part, prepares for the discussion to come; a major point in the discussion states the offering of the superior high priest is also superior due to its heavenly locale. Accordingly, the references in Heb. 8:2 to τῶν ἁγίων and τῆς σκηνῆς are the first in the book, but each plays a major role in the argument of 8:3-10:18.

Therefore, Heb. 8:1-2 functions as a direct intermediary transition between 5:1-7:28 and 8:3-10:18.[27] Elements of this unit belong

---

[27] Heb. 4:1-2 may also be considered a direct intermediary transition which moves the discussion from the negative example of those who fell in the wilderness through unbelief (3:12-17) to the topic of the promised rest for those who believe (4:3-11).

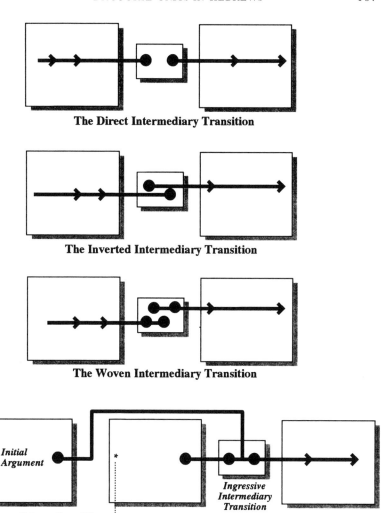

The Direct Intermediary Transition

The Inverted Intermediary Transition

The Woven Intermediary Transition

The Ingressive Intermediary Transition

Fig. 25. Patterns of intermediary transitions.

to the first section of material and other elements belong to the section which follows. This relationship is illustrated in fig. 26.

The Appointment of the Son as High Priest (5:1-7:28)

Κεφάλαιον δὲ ἐπὶ τοῖς λεγομένοις,
τοιοῦτον ἔχομεν ἀρχιερέα, ὃς ἐκάθισεν
ἐν δεξιᾷ τοῦ θρόνου τῆς μεγαλωσύνης
ἐν τοῖς οὐρανοῖς, τῶν ἁγίων λειτουργὸς
καὶ τῆς σκηνῆς τῆς ἀληθινῆς, ἣν
ἔπηξεν ὁ κύριος, οὐκ ἄνθρωπος
(8:1-2)

The Better, Heavenly offering in the True Tabernacle (8:3-10:18)

Fig. 26. Heb. 8:1-2 as a direct intermediary transition.

The Woven Intermediary Transition

Heb. 2:5-9 is another passage where the author makes use of *gezerah shawah*.[28] In Heb. 1:13 he quotes Ps. 110:1 which includes the phrase τῶν ποδῶν. The quote of Ps. 8:4-6 is brought into discussion by virtue of the same phrase τῶν ποδῶν from Ps. 8:6.

Use of this exegetical technique in Heb. 2:5-9 serves, in part, to raise a question concerning an apparent contradiction between the two passages. Have all things already been put under the Son's feet, as Ps. 8 suggests, or is the time of total subjection yet to come, as suggested in Ps. 110:1? The author's answer is that all things have been subjected to Him, but believers do not yet see this reality (v. 8).

Heb. 2:5-9 also serves another function. It forms an intermediary transition between the first main movement of the discourse on the Son's superiority to the angels (1:5-14), and the second concerning the necessity of the Son becoming lower than the angels (2:10-18). As seen in fig. 27, this intermediary transition is "woven" with elements from the two larger units by which it is flanked.

The concepts in Heb. 2:5-9 which relate to Heb. 1:5-14 center around the idea of subjection. These include the forms of ὑποτάσσω

---

[28] See the discussion supra, 67.

(vv. 5, 8), forms of στεφανόω (vv. 7, 9), and πάντα ὑπέταξας ὑποκάτω τῶν ποδων αὐτοῦ (v. 8). The key phrases that relate to what follows in 2:10-18 are ἠλάττωσας αὐτὸν βραχύ τι παρ᾿ ἀγγέλους (v. 7) and the repeating of that phrase in verse nine.

In Heb. 2:5-9 the author uses Ps. 8:4-6 to form the transition because it contains both references to the superiority of the Son (the topic of the preceding movement) as well as a reference to the temporary local subordination of the Son (the topic of the following movement) to the angels.

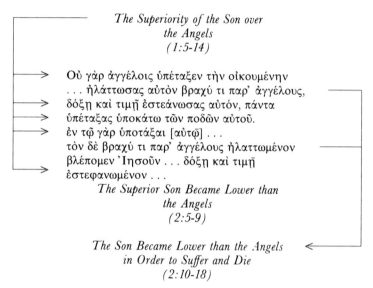

Fig. 27. Heb. 2:5-9 as a woven intermediary transition.

The common denominator between what precedes and what follows is the relationship of the Son to the angels. The author has already established the Son as higher than the angels (1:4-14). He now wishes to show, on the basis of Ps. 8:4-6, that it was necessary for the Son to become lower than the angels in order to accomplish man's salvation and be glorified as high priest. The reference to Ps. 8:4-6 in Heb. 2:5-9 moves the argument from the first point to the second. The transition, then, does not belong exclusively to either of the embedded discourse units but effects a transition between the two.

The Ingressive Intermediary Transition

It has been demonstrated that the author of Hebrews uses distant hook words to effect a connection between 5:1-10 and 7:1-10. The author also uses another transition device, labeled here the ingressive intermediary transition, to connect the two passages.

In Heb. 5:1-10 the author quotes Ps. 110:4 the first time. As the focal text in 5:1-10 it serves to show that Christ was appointed by God to be high priest. However, this verse plays a primary role in 7:1-28. The author uses it as a departing point to speak of the superiority of Melchizedek (7:1-10), the Melchizedekan "order" according to which Christ was appointed high priest (7:11-14), and the eternality of Christ's priesthood, utilizing the phrases εἰς τὸν αἰῶνα (7:15-17, 23-25) and Ὤμοσεν κύριος καὶ οὐ μεταμεληθήσεται (7:21-22).

All of Heb. 7:1-28 continues the discussion of Christ's appointment introduced in 5:1-10.[29] Yet the two units are separated by Heb. 5:11-6:20. The analyst may ask why the author breaks the continuity of his argument at this point.

Heb. 5:11-6:20 should be seen as a strategically placed digression from the discussion on the appointment of Christ as high priest.[30] The author himself intimates this in 5:11: Περὶ οὗ πολὺς ἡμῖν ὁ λόγος καὶ δυσερμήνευτος λέγειν, ἐπεὶ νωθροὶ γεγόνατε. He says there is much he wishes to say about Melchizedek, but then turns abruptly to address a pressing issue—the hearers' immaturity. This discussion of immaturity (5:11-14) and the need to press on to maturity (6:1-12) breaks off at Heb. 6:12, as the *inclusio* at 5:11/6:12 shows.[31]

Heb. 6:13-20 forms another intermediary transition. At the center of the passage stands the concept of God's "oath." The author's point concerns God's faithfulness to his declarations and the confidence which such faithfulness should afford Christians (6:17-20). What, then, is the oath of which the author speaks? It is Ps. 110:4, introduced at Heb. 5:6. This is the Old Testament verse associated with the ὀρκωμοσίας at 7:20-22. The author emphasizes both the

---

[29] In this regard see supra, 82 on the *inclusio* at Heb. 5:1-3/7:26-28.

[30] The term "digression" should not be taken to mean "less important." As will be demonstrated, Heb. 5:11-6:20 stands at the center of the author's purpose for the discourse.

[31] Supra, 83-84.

form of this psalm passage (note the second person singular pronoun) as well as the statement Ὤμοσεν κύριος καὶ οὐ μεταμεληθήσεται (Ps. 110:4a), introduced at 7:21.

It is this portion of the psalm which lies behind Heb. 6:17-18a. The "unchangeableness" (ἀμετάθετον) of God's purpose is shown by the fact that he has "sworn and will not change his mind" (Ps. 110:4). The δύο πραγμάτων ἀμεταθέτων of 6:18 are two parts of Ps. 110:4 which the author expounds in Hebrews 7. He is a priest εἰς τὸν αἰῶνα (7:15-25) and a priest appointed κατὰ τὴν τάξιν Μελχισέδεκ (7:11-14). These phrases from Ps. 110:4 explain the hope as ἀσφαλῆ τε καὶ βεβαίαν καὶ εἰσερχομένην εἰς τὸ ἐσώτερον τοῦ καταπετάσματος. The hope (6:18-19) is certain because Christ has been appointed to an unending priesthood. It enters within the veil because he is a high priest.

Therefore, Heb. 6:13-20 utilizes concepts from Ps. 110:4, first quoted at Heb. 5:6, in order to lead into the discussion of the Melchizedekan high priesthood of Christ. At the same time, however, these eight verses of Hebrews 6 flow from Heb. 6:12. The hearers can move from their sluggishness by imitating those who by faith and patience inherit God's promises. Therefore, Heb. 6:13-20 is "intermediary" in that it stands between 5:11-6:12 and 7:1-28 and is "ingressive" in that it leads out of the digression begun at Heb. 5:11.

Summary of Transition Techniques in Hebrews

The author of Hebrews uses no fewer than ten identifiable techniques for executing transitions in Hebrews. These are hook words, distant hook words, three types of hooked key words, overlapping constituents, parallel introductions, direct intermediary transitions, woven intermediary transitions, and an ingressive intermediary transition.

All of these techniques are significant for understanding the structure of Hebrews. The distant hook words, overlapping constituents, parallel introductions, and intermediary transitions are, however, most important for understanding the large picture of development in the book and the grouping of embedded discourses. These transition techniques play a central role in Chapter 7, an assessment of the functions of embedded discourse units in Hebrews.

CHAPTER SEVEN

THE STRUCTURE OF HEBREWS

Introduction

The analysis set forth in Chapters 5 and 6 serves to demonstrate basic forms of interrelatedness between discourse units in Hebrews. Identification of lexical and pronominal elements which build cohesion in the discourse, along with the author's uses of *inclusio*, have shown that Hebrews consists of hierarchically arranged groups of units. Use of transition devices, a special form of lexical cohesion, functions as a primary means for the author to effect movement between units.

However, any investigation of the structure of Hebrews has as its ultimate goal an elucidation of the logic behind the organization of paragraphs into embedded discourses and embedded discourses into a coherent macro-discourse. The critic must examine why the author arranged his material as he did. The present chapter, therefore, seeks an answer to this question, bringing the study to its *raison d'être*. Foremost, a distinction must be made between the units of exposition and those of exhortation.

Why Expositional and Hortatory Units Must, Initially, be Considered Separately

Distinguishing between the forms and purposes of expositional and hortatory units in a text has long been a basic aspect of New Testament exegesis and interpretation.[1] Commentators note, for example, that most of Paul's letters may be easily divided into an expositional, or theological, part with which he begins a book, and a hortatory part, with which he ends the book.[2] These parts each play complementary roles in the overall purpose of the letter.

---

[1] Aune, *The New Testament in Its Literary Environment*, 191-97; Berger, *Exegese des Neuen Testaments*, 15, 36-58.
[2] The exceptions here are 1-2 Corinthians and Philippians. See Aune, *The New Testament in its Literary Environment*, 191.

Obviously, however, from numerous discussions on the structure of Hebrews, the layout of this book disallows any simple bipartite scheme. Rather, the author shifts back and forth between exposition and exhortation; this phenomenon has raised the question of the relationship between these two predominant genres in Hebrews. Does the author use the hortatory material as merely a stylistic digression from his theological treatise, or does the expositional material in some way serve to lay the foundation for the author's main goal of exhortation?[3]

As noted in Chapter 1, Albert Vanhoye, following the earlier works of F. Büchsel and Rafael Gyllenberg, used "change in genre" as an important literary indicator by which discernment of the structure of Hebrews might be facilitated.[4] The rationale behind this procedure is that a change in genre marks some shift in the discourse. The author changes from expositional comments on christological themes to addressing his hearers directly. The hortatory pericopes, therefore, are set apart as distinct from the expositional pericopes.

This practice of stressing a fine demarcation between the expositional and hortatory material in Hebrews has drawn fire from scholars such as Wolfgang Nauck, Werner Georg Kümmel, Otto Michel, and H. Zimmermann.[5] Criticism has been leveled on at least two bases.

First, Vanhoye, Gyllenberg, Büchsel, and others center their outlines around the expositional (i.e., christological) material in the book. Headings of the main sections of the outline are derived from the expositional material. Such outlines leave the impression that the author's main goal was instruction concerning certain aspects of christology.[6]

---

[3] This question concerning Hebrews really constitutes part of the larger "Indicative-Imperative" debate in New Testament studies. For a balanced analysis of Hebrews as it relates to that debate see Übelacker, *Der Hebräerbrief als Appell*, 17, 32-36.

[4] Supra, 34. James Swetnam, who criticizes Vanhoye, yet follows his lead on a number of points, also uses the change from exposition to exhortation and back as a primary indicator of the structure of the book. See Swetnam, "Form and Content in Hebrews 7-13," 344-45.

[5] Nauck, "Zum Aufbau des Hebräerbriefes," 201-203; Kümmel, *Introduction to the New Testament*, 390; Michel, *Der Brief an die Hebräer*, 29-35; Zimmermann, *Das Bekenntnis der Hoffnung*, 17-24.

[6] The work of James Swetnam and the later formulations of Vanhoye do a better job of reflecting the hortatory purpose of the hortatory blocks of material in the

Nauck, Michel, Zimmermann, and Kümmel, on the other hand, suggest it is the paraenesis which stands at the center of the author's purpose.[7] These scholars understand the primary aim of Hebrews, a self-described "word of exhortation" (13:22), to be to challenge the new "wandering people of God" to continue their journey to the heavenly Jerusalem.[8] The author, they believe, uses both the expositional and hortatory sections to that end. They view the expositional material as the basis for exhortation. The hortatory goal of the exposition is skewed when too sharp a differentiation is made between the two genres. Thus, in the tripartite scheme of Nauck, who is followed by Kümmel, the titles of the three major sections of the book are worded so as to reflect the hortatory goal of the author: "*Hear* the Word of God in the Son" (1:1-4:13), "*Let Us Approach* the High Priest" (4:14-10:31), and "*Hold Fast* to Jesus Christ" (10:32-13:17).[9]

Second, closely related to the first criticism, Nauck suggests that hortatory blocks of material play the primary role in framing structurally the three major divisions of Hebrews. For example, he notes that the author uses parallel passages at 4:14-16 and 10:19-31 to bracket (or form an *inclusio* around) the central section of the book. Therefore, these hortatory units frame the exposition from 5:1-10:18, producing a unified movement stretching from 4:14 all the way to 10:31.[10] To draw a line of separation between 4:14-16 and the exposition which follows, or between 10:19-31 and the exposition which precedes it, is to disjoin that which was intended to be a unified section of the discourse.[11] Nauck's criticisms are valid and

book. See Swetnam, "Form and Content in Hebrews 7-13," 344-45; Vanhoye, "Literarische Struktur und theologische Botschaft des Hebräerbriefs (1. Teil)," 142-43.

[7] Nauck, "Zum Aufbau des Hebräerbriefes," 201-203; Kümmel, *Introduction to the New Testament*, 390; Michel, *Der Brief an die Hebräer*, 29-35; Zimmermann, *Das Bekenntnis der Hoffnung*, 17-24. See also Schierse, *Verheißung und Heilsvollendung*, 207-209; Black, "The Problem of the Literary Structure of Hebrews," 166-67; Lindars, "The Rhetorical Structure of Hebrews," 394-97.

[8] Erich Grässer sees Ernst Käsemann's 1938 publication *Das wandernde Gottesvolk: Eine Untersuchung zum Hebräerbrief* as a turning point in the study of Hebrews since it shifted the focus of study on the book to the paraenetic sections. See Grässer, "Der Hebräerbrief 1938-1963," 144.

[9] Nauck, "Zum Aufbau des Hebräerbriefes," 203-206.

[10] Ibid., 200-203.

[11] Vanhoye and Swetnam have not been entirely consistent in dividing the book on the basis of these two genres. For example, in his earlier work Vanhoye designated all of 4:15-5:10 as "doctrinal," although 4:15-16 is obviously hortatory. In

champion the position that exhortation and exposition in Hebrews must be considered for their interaction. When these two genres are held too far apart and the important hortatory passages are lost in an expositionally oriented outline, the overall purpose of Hebrews is skewed.

Nevertheless, one can criticize Nauck and his followers on at least two points. First, a noticeable difference in form does exist between the expository and hortatory sections of Hebrews. With the switch to exhortation, the temporal frame of reference changes from the past to the present, and the author turns to address directly his hearers.[12]

Second, demonstrated under consideration of transitions in Hebrews, the author uses distant hook words to link units of the same genre separated by intervening units of a different genre.[13] This suggestion raises the possibility that the author points to some semantic continuation between units of the same genre that is not shared by intervening units of the other genre. This does not mean that no semantic continuation exists when the author changes from one genre to the next. It merely suggests potential benefit in considering the unique semantic program of each genre in Hebrews before trying to discern their joint venture.

To insist that the two genres must not be held apart in structural analyses of the book is important but insufficient. Why the author alternates between these two forms must be investigated and the unique function of each ascertained. While it may be true that

---

his later formulations he corrected this error. Swetnam labeled all of 3:1-6:20 as "exhortation" although 5:1-11 contains expositional material. See Swetnam, "Form and Content in Hebrews 7-13," 344; Vanhoye, *La structure littéraire de l'Épître aux Hébreux*, 59; idem., "Literarische Struktur und theologische Botschaft des Hebräerbriefs (1. Teil)," 142.

[12] Hartwig Thyen's study on the style of the Jewish-hellenistic synagogue sermon emphasizes this fact. In chapter three of his monograph, entitled "Form und Komposition der Paränesen," Thyen demonstrates numerous characteristics common to the paraenetic sections of Jewish-Hellenistic synagogue homilies, including the communicative "we" (over against the general use of the third person), the use of ἀδελφοί to address the hearers, use of διό, διὰ τοῦτο, or οὖν to make a transition from exposition to an exhortation, use of the second person singular or plural to directly address the hearers (and shift between "I" and "you"), a personal warm tone, the use of *exempla*, and an apocalyptic background to the thoughts being expressed. See *Der Stil des jüdisch-hellenistischen Homilie*, 85-110.

[13] Supra, 96-100.

exhortation and exposition in the book are intertwined in accomplishing the overall purpose of the author, the unique roles of each in accomplishing that purpose need attention. The difference in form raises the possibility of some difference in function between the two *Gattungen*.[14] Nauck's scheme in no way addresses this possibility.[15]

Since the specialized functions of each of the two main genres in Hebrews must first be discerned before assessment of their interaction can be clarified, the analysis involves three stages. First, the relationships between units of exposition are scrutinized. Second, investigation focuses on hortatory passages. Finally, conclusions are drawn concerning the interaction of exposition with exhortation in accomplishing the author's overall purpose for the discourse. In the present chapter, discussion of the semantic program of individual units, inclusions, and transition devices is based on the detailed analysis set forth in Chapters 4 through 6 of this study.

ARRANGEMENT OF EXPOSITIONAL UNITS IN HEBREWS

The author's exposition, outlined in fig. 28, may be divided into an introduction followed by two main movements. The first of these main movements deals with "The Position of the Son in Relation to the Angels," which runs from Heb. 1:5 through 2:18. The second runs from Heb. 4:14 through 10:25 with an exposition on "The Position of the Son, Our High Priest, in Relation to the Earthly Sacrificial System." The first embedded discourse has one hortatory unit breaking the clear flow of exposition. The second embedded discourse is briefly interrupted by the hortatory digression at 5:11-6:20.

---

[14] For the various functions of paraenesis in early Christian literature see Aune, *The New Testament in Its Literary Environment*, 189-97.

[15] Whereas Vanhoye failed to give adequate representation of hortatory material in his scheme, Nauck and followers are in danger of committing the same error with regard to the expositional material in the book. Large sections of Hebrews consist of the author's expositions of Old Testament texts. These expositions *are* christologically oriented and seem to be intended to instruct the hearers. Even if these sections do serve as foundation for the hortatory material in the book, as Nauck suggests, their unique pedagogical function in the development of the book should be reflected in an outline of Hebrews.

INTRODUCTION: GOD HAS SPOKEN TO US IN A SON (1:1-4)

I.   THE POSITION OF THE SON IN RELATION TO THE AN-
     GELS (1:5-2:18)

     A.   The Son Superior to the Angels (1:5-14)

     ab. The Superior Son for a Time Became Positionally Lower than
          the Angels (2:5-9)

     B.   The Son Lower than the Angels (i.e., among men) to Suffer
          for the sons (2:10-18)

II. THE POSITION OF THE SON, OUR HIGH PRIEST, IN RE-
     LATION TO THE EARTHLY SACRIFICIAL SYSTEM (4:14-
     10:25)

     OPENING: WE HAVE A SINLESS HIGH PRIEST WHO HAS
     GONE INTO HEAVEN (4:14-16)

     A.   The Appointment of the Son as a Superior High Priest (5:1-
          10, 7:1-28)

          1.   Introduction: The Son Taken from Among Men and Appointed
               According to the Order of Melchizedek (5:1-10)

          2.   The Superiority of Melchizedek (7:1-10)

          3.   The Superiority of Our Eternal, Melchizedekan High Priest
               (7:11-28)

     ab. We Have Such a High Priest Who is a Minister in Heaven
          (8:1-2)

     B.   The Superior Offering of the Appointed High Priest (8:3-
          10:18)

          1.   Introduction: The More Excellent Ministry of the Heavenly
               High Priest (8:3-6)

          2.   The Superiority of the New Covenant (8:7-13)

          3.   The Superior New Covenant Offering (9:1-10:18)

     CLOSING: WE HAVE A GREAT PRIEST WHO TAKES US
     INTO HEAVEN (10:19-25)

Fig. 28. Outline of expositional material in Hebrews.

INTRODUCTION: GOD HAS SPOKEN TO US IN A SON (HEB. 1:1-4)

In ancient Greek oratory and Jewish homiletics great emphasis was placed on a piece having an appropriate introduction, otherwise known as an *exordium*, or *proem*. For example, the Jewish "proem midrash" form was introduced with a reference to the text to be expounded.[16] In Greek oratory the first division of a speech was the *exordium*, crafted with the intent of gaining the audience's attention and introducing the central topics to be covered.[17]

Heb. 1:1-4 has been called "an obvious and commonly accepted division,"[18] and, indeed, most commentators have set it apart as the introduction to the book.[19] These four verses form a single, multi-clause sentence built on "periodic style."[20] To the author's use of periodism in this passage may be added effectiveness, compactness, contrast, cohesion, poetic structure, omissions, figures, repetition (alliteration), rhythm, and semitisms.[21] In these first four verses the author uses an elaborate display of rhetorical devices to gain his audience's attention.

Furthermore, this highly stylized combination of clauses and phrases introduces the topics "God," "the Son," "the word of God," "the hearers being addressed," "the heavenly sphere," "inheritance," "purification of sins," "angels," and "the Son as 'bet-

---

[16] Borgen, *Bread From Heaven*, 59-98. E. Earle Ellis, "Isaiah in the New Testament," *Southwestern Journal of Theology* 34 (1991): 31-32.

[17] Watson, *Invention, Arrangement, and Style*, 21; Clark, Donald L., *Rhetoric in Greco-Roman Education* (Morningside Heights, NY: Columbia University Press, 1957), 112-13; Russell and Winterbottom, *Ancient Literary Criticism*, 170; Lausberg, *Handbuch der Literarischen Rhetorik*, 148-51; Volkmann, *Die Rhetorik der Griechen und Römer*, 127-29.

[18] Swetnam, "Form and Content in Hebrews 1-6," 372.

[19] E.g., Michel, *Der Brief an die Hebräer*, 92; Bruce, *The Epistle to the Hebrews*, lxiii-lxiv.

[20] A "period" is a highly stylized configuration of clauses and phrases which concludes with an appropriate and majestic ending. "Periodic style" was considered artistic and contrasted with "loose," or "free running" prose. With periodic style the sentence had a definite beginning and a definite ending. While "loose" style was acceptable in historical and narrative prose, periodic style was commonly used in oratory. The substance of the period was often built around either similarity or contrast between sets of clauses, as is the case in Heb. 1:1-2. See Russell and Winterbottom, eds., *Ancient Literary Criticism*, 175-79; Clark, *Rhetoric in Greco-Roman Education*, 97-99; J. W. H. Atkins, *Literary Criticism in Antiquity: A Sketch of its Development* (Gloucester, MA: Peter Smith, 1961), 33; F. Blass and A. Debrunner, *A Greek Grammar of the New Testament and Other Early Christian Literature*, trans. Robert W. Funk (Chicago: University of Chicago Press, 1961), 242.

[21] So Black, "Hebrews 1:1-4: A Study in Discourse Analysis," 181-92.

ter'," which constitute the most important concepts in the discourse.[22]

With its majestic style and high concentration of programmatic topics, which the author will elaborate throughout the book, Heb. 1:1-4 may be identified as the "introduction" of the discourse.[23] As such it will have relevance for both the hortatory and the expository material. Beginning with the relative clause in Heb. 1:2b, the author focuses the introduction on the Son, "who sat down at the right hand of the Majesty" (1:3). That focus remains throughout the balance of the expositional material.

I. The Position of the Son in Relation to the Angels (Heb. 1:5-2:18)
The exposition found in Heb. 1:5-2:18 revolves around the contrast between the Son and the angels. It may be divided into two subsections separated by the intermediary transition at 2:5-9. Using a chain of texts to show the Son's exalted position, the author presents "The Son Superior to the Angels" in Heb. 1:5-14. The quote of Ps. 8:4-6 in the intermediary transition (2:5-9) is introduced by virtue of its verbal analogy with Ps. 110:1, the two texts sharing the common phrase τῶν ποδῶν. This quote of Ps. 8:4-6 serves to move the discussion to a consideration of the incarnation. The Son became "lower" than the angels, partaking of flesh, being made like his brothers, in order to suffer on their behalf and deliver them. Since discussion of the Son's incarnation departs from the ἠλάττωσας αὐτὸν βραχύ τι παρ' ἀγγέλους of Ps. 5-6, Heb. 2:10-18 may be given the title "The Son Lower Than the Angels (i.e., "among men") to Suffer for the sons" (2:10-18).

Therefore, the exposition at Heb. 1:5-2:18 moves from proclamation of the Son's superiority (1:5-14), through the transition showing the superior one became lower (2:5-9), to a discussion of the incarnation (2:10-18).

II. The Position of the Son, Our High Priest, in Relation to the Earthly Sacrificial System (Heb. 4:14-10:25)
In the discussion of inclusions in Chapter 5, the elaborate *inclusio* at 4:14-16/10:19-25 marks the great central section of the book.[24]

---

[22] Supra, 91-94.

[23] The most extensive study to date on Heb. 1:1-4 as an *exordium* has been carried out by Walter Übelacker. See *Der Hebräerbrief als Appell*, 66-138.

[24] Supra, 79-82.

While the units at 4:14-16 and 10:19-25 are hortatory, they have
been shown to function in a special relationship to the expositional
material in Hebrews.[25] Therefore, among the hortatory units in the
book they must be given special consideration in the present discussion on expositional material.

The opening at Heb. 4:14-16 affirms that believers have ἀρχιερέα
μέγαν διεληλυθότα τοὺς οὐρανούς. The great central section closes at
10:19-25 with the proclamation that the great priest has won believers entrance into heaven. These thoughts contain the essence of the
author's argument in Heb. 5:1-10:18.

Like Heb. 1:5-2:18, so Heb. 5:1-10:18 can be divided into two
subsections separated by an intermediary transition. The first of
these subsections, 5:1-7:28, is bracketed by the *inclusio* at 5:1-3/7:26-
28 and deals with "The Appointment of the Son as a Superior High
Priest." The second subsection, 8:3-10:18, expounds "The Superior
Offering of the Appointed High Priest," and is also marked by an
inclusio at 8:3/10:18. These two embedded discourses are separated
by the intermediary transition at 8:1-2.

Furthermore, Heb. 5:1-7:28 and 8:3-10:18 may each be divided
into three smaller, corresponding subsections. "The Appointment
of the Son as a Superior High Priest" begins with an introduction
(5:1-10), continues with a section on Melchizedek's superiority to
the Levitical priesthood (7:1-10), and ends with proclamation of
Christ's superiority to the Levitical priesthood based on Ps. 110:4
(7:11-28).

"The Superior Offering of the Appointed High Priest" begins
with an introduction (8:3-6), the first verse forming a "parallel introduction" with Heb. 5:1. Quoting Jer. 31:31-34, the author asserts "The Superiority of the New Covenant" in Heb. 8:7-13, and
then follows with an extensive treatment of "The Superior New
Covenant Offering" in 9:1-10:18.

Thus, in each of the two primary embedded discourses of Heb.
5:1-10:18 an introduction is followed by the demonstration of an
institution's superiority to the old covenant priesthood based on
Old Testament proof texts. Building on the latter, the author then

---

[25] These units present an overlapping constituents transition (supra, 102-104)
between the hortatory and expositional material in the book, and, unlike other
hortatory units in the book, are connected to a previous expositional unit by distant hook words (supra, 96-100).

sets forth the superiority of Christ's ministry. Therefore, "IIA1" of the outline in fig. 28 above corresponds to "IIB1," "IIA2" corresponds to "IIB2," and "IIA3" corresponds to "IIB3."[26]

"The Superior New Covenant Offering" (9:1-10:18) may be subdivided further into three movements: 9:1-10, 9:11-28, and 10:1-18. Heb. 9:1-10 presents the regulations for worship under the old covenant. Under this old system the high priest's offering involved blood (9:7), was made in the earthly sanctuary (9:1), and took place once a year (9:7). These three concepts are developed in 9:11-10:18 by way of contrast to Jesus' superior ministry (δέ is used to show the contrast at 9:11). With *his own blood* Christ entered into the *heavenly sanctuary* (9:11-28). There he offered one offering effective *for all time*, never to be repeated (10:1-18).

Development of the Argument

The expositional units of Hebrews fall into two primary embedded discourses: the first dealing with "The Position of the Son in Relation to the Angels" (1:5-2:18), and the second "The Position of the Son, Our High Priest, in Relation to the Earthly Sacrificial System" (4:14-10:25). Moreover, these embedded discourses each may be divided into two smaller embedded discourses. IA sets forth "The Son Superior to the Angels" (1:5-14) and IB "The Son Lower than the Angels" (2:10-18). "The Appointment of the Son as a Superior High Priest" constitutes IIA, while "The Superior Offering of the Appointed High Priest" is dealt with in IIB.

Rather than merely representing a loose association of topics, however, these four primary movements of the expositional material develop from one unit to the next. This development is both spatial and logical.

The Argument is Spatial

In Hebrews an emphasis on spatial orientation to either heaven or earth resides primarily in the expositional material.[27] As depicted in

---

[26] Note also that IIA3 and IIB3 each begin with the construction μὲν οὖν, only found elsewhere in Hebrews at 8:4.

[27] E.g., references to the heavenly sphere: 1:3,13; 2:10; 4:14; 6:19-20; 7:26; 8:1; 8:5; 9:11-12,23-24; 10:12; 12:2,22,23,25; references to the earthly sphere: 1:6; 2:7,9,12,14,17; 8:4; 9:1,11; 10:5; 12:25. The exceptions are the transitions at 4:14 and 6:19-20 and the material in Heb. 12:1-25.

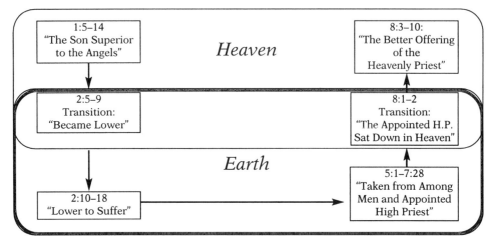

Fig. 29. Spatial movement in the expositional development of Hebrews.

fig. 29, the intermediary transitions found at Heb. 2:5-9 and 8:1-2
serve to move the discussion from one sphere to the other.

The discourse begins with the exalted status of the Son over the
angels (1:5-14). At Heb. 2:5-9, however, the author makes a spatial
transition to the earthly sphere in order to focus on the Son's solidarity with, and suffering for, mankind (2:10-18). The exposition
continues with "The Appointment of the Son as a Superior High
Priest" (5:1-7:28). In 5:1-7:28 the author focuses on the permanence of Christ's priesthood, especially playing off God's "oath"
(Ὤμοσεν κύριος καὶ οὐ μεταμεληθήσεται) and the phrase εἰς τὸν
αἰῶνα, both from Ps. 110:4. While spatial orientation is not primary
here, the section begins with high priests in general being taken ἐξ
ἀνθρώπων.

Spatial concerns are foregrounded again with reference to ἐν τοῖς
οὐρανοῖς at the intermediary transition of Heb. 8:1-2.[28] The dis-

---

The pattern of God's Son leaving heaven, coming to earth to suffer and die for
humanity, and then being exalted back to heaven finds expression at various places
in early Christian literature. Of special interest is Phil. 2:5-11. See Attridge, *The
Epistle to the Hebrews*, 78-81; Martin Hengel, *The Son of God* (Philadelphia: Fortress
Press, 1976), 87. Attridge correctly finds fault with Käsemann's thesis that the
incarnational christology of Hebrews conforms to the pattern of the Gnostic re-
deemer myth. See Käsemann, *The Wandering People of God*, 101.

[28] The reference to τῶν οὐρανῶν in 7:26 is a "hooked key word" foreshadowing
entrance into the next section.

cussion remains in the heavenly realm throughout the rest of the expositional material, the heavenly sacrifice of the new high priest being set over against the earthly sacrificial system.

Of special interest here is the author's uses of Ps. 110:1.[29] First, the initial spatial reference in the book is found in the author's reference to the *Session* ἐν ὑψηλοῖς at Heb. 1:3. This allusion to Ps. 110:1 turns the discourse toward the first movement of the book on "The Son Higher than the Angels" (1:5-14), as is shown by the syntactic dependence of Heb. 1:4 on the verb ἐκάθισεν. The allusion to Ps. 110:1 at Heb. 1:3, therefore, provides the spatial point of reference with which the book begins.

Second, the quote of Ps. 110:1 at Heb. 1:13 provides a spatial point of reference for the author's transition to his next section. By virtue of the phrase τῶν ποδῶν in Ps. 110:1 the author adds Ps. 8:4-6, which also contains the phrase.[30] The "subjection to the Son" theme inherent in Ps. 110:1 gives rise to Ps. 8:4-6 being used to make a transition to the next topic of discussion.

The discourse, as explained earlier, stays in the earthly realm until the intermediary transition at Heb. 8:1-2. In 8:1 allusion is once again made to Ps. 110:1. Now, however, the ἐν ὑψηλοῖς of 1:3 is replaced with ἐν τοῖς οὐρανοῖς. The purpose of this redaction is once again to provide the reader with a spatial point of reference "in the heavens." This point of reference is needed because one of the author's main arguments concerning the superiority of Christ's offering (8:3-10:18) has to do with it being made *in heaven*.

Finally, the fourth reference to Ps. 110:1 (Heb. 10:12) comes at the end of "The Superior Offering of the Appointed High Priest" (8:3-10:18). This allusion serves a temporal function by demonstrating the finality of the Son's sacrifice. Yet, it also serves to provide spatial movement, the heavenly high priest moving from the heavenly altar to the heavenly throne, where he will remain until his enemies are made a footstool for his feet.

Therefore, the allusion to Ps. 110:1 in Heb. 1:3 initiates the spatial orientation to the heavenly realm, the quote at 1:13 and the allusion at 8:1 provide means for major spatial transitions in the

---

[29] George H. Guthrie, "Exaltation Theology in Hebrews: A Discourse Analysis of the Function of Psalm 110:1 in Hebrews 1:3," (Master's thesis, Trinity Evangelical Divinity School, 1989), 117-19.

[30] Supra, 108.

discourse, while the allusion at 10:12 offers the spatial end point for
the expositional material. The Son begins and ends sitting at the
right hand of God.

The Argument as Logical

For the author of Hebrews the movement from one point in the
expositional argument to the next is more than merely spatially
oriented. It is logically built around *midrashim* of Old Testament
texts.[31]

As already noted, Ps. 110:1 is the final quote in the *haraz* of Hebrews 1 (1:13) and by verbal analogy semantically links with the
quote of Ps. 8:4-6 at Heb. 2:6-8. The concept of the Son of Man
being made "lower" (Ps. 8:5) is supplemented by texts reflecting the
association of the Son with the sons (2:12-13).[32]

---

[31] So Caird, "The Exegetical Method of the Epistle to the Hebrews," 44-51;
John Walters, "The Rhetorical Arrangement of Hebrews," in correspondence to
George H. Guthrie, 24 July 1991; E. Earle Ellis, *The Old Testament in Early Christianity* (Tübingen: J. C. B. Mohr [Paul Siebeck], 1991), 96-101, passim.
    There is somewhat of a current dilemma in defining and delimiting the term
"midrash". The Hebrew word itself (מדרש), a cognate of the verb דרש, meaning to
"inquire about" or "examine", basically means "commentary." Before the 1950's
it was primarily used to designate certain rabbinic commentaries on the Old Testament. More recently, however, the term has been used to refer to *the activity of
exposition* as well as the resulting literary genre. The essence of the *practice* of midrash
involved the citation of a text, or texts, followed by exposition, often with reference
to secondary texts. E. Earle Ellis states that the midrashic pattern
    takes various forms. It may appear as a cluster of texts and commentary on a
    particular theme, similar to the *florilegia* found at Qumran, or as a special
    pattern. More frequently, it occurs in literary forms found in rabbinic exposi-
    tions, the 'proem' and '*yelammedenu rabbenu*' ('let our master teach us') mi-
    drashim. While in the rabbinic collections these forms date from several centu-
    ries after the New Testament, they were hardly borrowed from the Christians.
    Also, similar patterns are present in the first-century Jewish writer, Philo. One
    may infer then, with some confidence, that their presence in the New Testa-
    ment reflects a common, rather widespread Jewish usage.
See Ellis, *The Old Testament in Early Christianity*, 96.
    On the use of midrash also see M. P. Miller, "Targum, Midrash and the Use of
the Old Testament in the New Testament," *Journal for the Study of Judaism* 2 (1970):
37; Martin McNamara, "Some Issues and Recent Writings on Judaism and the
NT," *Irish Biblical Studies* 9 (1987): 136-49; E. Earle Ellis, *Prophesy and Hermeneutic in
Early Christianity*, Wissenschaftliche Untersuchungen zum Neuen Testament (Tübingen: J. C. B. Mohr [Paul Siebeck], 1978), 151; *Dictionnaire de la Bible, Supplement*
(Paris, 1957), s.v. "Midrash," by Renée Bloch; R. Le Déaut, "A propos d'une
définition du midrash," *Biblica* 50 (1969): 395-413. Le Déaut counters Addison G.
Wright's attempt to limit a definition of midrash to literary genre. For Wright's
proposal see *Midrash: The Literary Genre* (New York: Alba House, 1967), 66.
[32] Note especially the reference to ἐν μέσῳ in the quote at Heb. 2:12.

According to Hebrews' author, the incarnation of the Son was a logical prerequisite for the Son's glorification and his deliverance of the sons. At Heb. 2:9 it is clear that the author takes the phrases ἠλάττωσας αὐτὸν βραχύ τι παρ' ἀγγέλους and δόξῃ καὶ τιμῇ ἐστεφάνωσας αὐτόν to be sequential, stating it was διὰ τὸ πάθημα τοῦ θανάτου that the one who became lower was δόξῃ καὶ τιμῇ ἐστεφανωμένον. Also, through his perfection (via sufferings), a concept associated with his being "lower" (e.g., Heb. 5:7-10), the Son would be able to bring "many sons to glory" (2:10). He *had* to take on flesh and blood in identification with the sons that through death he might bring the sons deliverance (2:14-15). This necessity is restated in Heb. 2:17-18 with ὤφειλεν κατὰ πάντα τοῖς ἀδελφοῖς ὁμοιωθῆναι, ἵνα ἐλεήμων γένηται καὶ πιστὸς ἀρχιερεὺς . . . The Son had to become lower than the angels in order to be made a superior high priest, who has been tempted through sufferings and can, therefore, aid those who are tempted. Here the author begins his transition to the next major expositional movement on "The Position of the Son, Our High Priest, in relation to the Earthly Sacrificial System" (4:14-10:25).[33]

As with every priest, the Son was taken ἐξ ἀνθρώπων (Heb. 5:1) and appointed to his position. He is, however, a very different kind of high priest—one who has been appointed with an oath. At Heb. 5:5-6 the author uses *gezerah shawah* to associate Ps. 2:7 and Ps. 110:4 (the *Stichwort* is σύ), thus making a transition from the material primarily concerned with "sonship" (1:5-2:18) to that focused on "high priesthood" (4:14-10:25). The focal text is Ps. 110:4: Σὺ ἱερεὺς εἰς τὸν αἰῶνα κατὰ τὴν τάξιν Μελχισέδεκ.

After the hortatory digression of Heb. 5:11-6:20, the author first shows the superiority of Melchizedek to the Levitical priesthood (7:1-10). To do this he supplements his original reference to Ps. 110:4 with a midrash on Gen. 14:17-20, the only other Old Testament passage which speaks of the enigmatic priest.[34] He then returns to Ps. 110:4 and, based on the phrases εἰς τὸν αἰῶνα and Ὤμοσεν κύριος καὶ οὐ μεταμεληθήσεται taken from that verse

---

[33] On the use of distant hook words connecting Heb. 2:17-18 to 4:14-16 and 5:1-3 see supra, 96-100.

[34] See Fitzmyer, "'Now this Melchizedek' (Heb. 7:1)," 306. Fitzmyer points out that Heb. 7:1-10 resembles the midrash in *Genesis Rabbah* 43:6.

proves that the Son's priesthood is superior to that of the Levitical priests because it will never end (7:11-28).

The "appointment" (5:1-7:28), of course, precedes the priest's offering sacrifice and is a logical prerequisite for that sacrifice. In fact, the purpose of the appointment is for the high priest to make sacrifice (5:1; 8:3).

The proclamation of the Son's appointment as high priest gives rise to a fresh allusion to Ps. 110:1 (in the intermediary transition of Heb. 8:1-2) and the quote of Jer. 31:31-34 (Heb. 8:8-12).[35] Based on these texts, plus allusions to various passages from the Torah (Heb. 9:1-22), and the quote of Ps. 40:6-8 (10:5-7),[36] the author expounds the superiority of the new covenant (8:7-13), then the superiority of Christ's offering under the new covenant (9:1-10:18). His logic is that the appointed Son's offering, as the new covenant offering of the superior priest, finds its superiority in its heavenly locale (9:11,23-24), the high priest's shed blood (9:12-22), and its permanence (10:1-18).

The expositional units in Hebrews, therefore, may be said to develop logically, the central propositions of each unit building on those expositional units which have gone before. This logical development is depicted in fig. 30. Furthermore, a primary means of moving the discussion from one major section to the next is his use of *gezerah shawah*, texts being added to the discussion by their verbal analogy with previously cited texts.

The Function of Expositional Units in Hebrews

The expositional units in Hebrews develop step-by-step, both spatially and logically. This tightly knit exposition serves to build the hearers' knowledge about the Son (or reminds them of facts they have known in the past). The author wishes to bring the Son into sharper focus by explicating relevant Old Testament passages

[35] Again *gezerah shawah* is used in making the transition by virtue of the *Stichwort* κύριος in Psalm 110 and Jer. 31:31.
[36] This passage has a verbal analogy with Jeremiah 31 through the common reference to ἁμαρτία (Jer. 31:34; Ps. 40:6). The reference to "sins" and "covenant" in Jer. 31:33-34 (quoted at Heb. 8:10-12) also leads to the allusions to Old Testament Torah texts on the sacrificial system. On the midrashic pattern of this section see Ellis, *The Old Testament in Early Christianity*, 107.

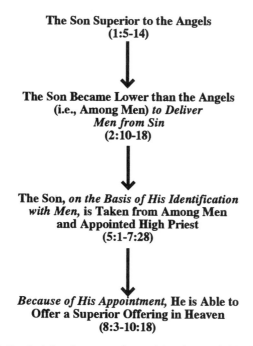

Fig. 30. Logical development of expositional material in Hebrews.

which show the Son's superiority to the angels (1:5-14), the purpose of his incarnation (2:10-18), the superiority of his priesthood (5:1-7:28), and the superiority of his offering as high priest (8:3-10:18).

AN ANALYSIS OF THE HORTATORY UNITS IN HEBREWS

In contradistinction from the expositional material, the semantic program of the hortatory units in Hebrews does not develop in a step-by-step argument, beginning at point x and moving systematically to point y.[37] Rather, the hortatory aim of the discourse is executed by reiteration of certain key topics. The study first considers the units individually, briefly providing an overview of each unit's message. Then the cohesive elements linking the hortatory units are evaluated. For now, intermediary and overlapping transitions at 4:1-2, 4:14-16, 6:13-20, and 10:19-25 are bracketed.

---

[37] This does not mean, of course, that no logical development occurs in the hortatory material, e.g., the movement from 3:12-19 to 4:3-11 (supra, 67).

Introduction: God has Spoken to Us in a Son
(Heb. 1:1-4)

The introductory nature of Heb. 1:1-4 has already been established.[38] In his *exordium* the author introduces key elements which are expressed throughout the balance of the hortatory material. These are "God," "the word of God," "the Son," and references to the members of the Christian community. God has spoken his word to the community through the Son.

Warning: Do Not Reject the Word
Spoken Through God's Son!
(Heb. 2:1-4)

In Heb. 2:1-4 the author presents his first strong warning to his hearers, addressing them directly concerning their responsibility as those blessed with the divine message of salvation. The exhortation coheres around an *a fortiori* argument: If the Son is greater than the angels and the rejection of the word of God delivered through the angels brought punishment, then rejection of the word of God delivered through the Son deserves even greater punishment.[39]

Jesus, the Supreme Example of a Faithful Son
(Heb. 3:1-6)

Although Heb. 3:1-6 has often been designated "Jesus Greater than Moses," the faithfulness of Jesus constitutes the prominent theme in the unit. The comparison with Moses serves to show the greater honor due Jesus. Moses was faithful as a servant, but "servant faithfulness" does not attain the status of "sonship faithfulness." Furthermore, this faithfulness of the Son serves as an example to the Christian community which, by holding to courage and hope, makes up "God's house." The implication is that the Christian community must also be faithful to God.

---

[38] Supra, 118-19.
[39] Supra, 62.

The Negative Example of Those
Who Fell Through Disobedience
(Heb. 3:7-19)

Heb. 3:7-19 forms a midrashic treatment of Ps. 95:7-11. The section consists of an introductory quote of Ps. 95 (3:7-11), an exhortation built around the concepts of unbelief, hardness of heart, and rebellion taken from the quote (3:12-14), and an elaboration of motifs found in the quote (3:15-19). Other Old Testament texts which may lie behind Heb. 3:12-19 are Ps. 106, Num. 14:1-38, Ps. 78, and Deut. 9.[40] The author sets before his hearers a graphic example of the cost of faithlessness. Those who test and turn away from God, hardening their hearts through sin and unbelief, face the anger of God.

The Promise of Rest for those who are Obedient
(Heb. 4:3-11)

At 4:3-11 Hebrews' author moves from the focus on punishment to a focus on the reward of κατάπαυσις. Introducing Gen. 2:2 (4:4) by virtue of its verbal analogy with Ps. 95:7-11 (the common reference to "rest"), he argues the rest rejected by those who fell in the wilderness may still be attained by those who are obedient.[41] That rest was first mentioned with reference to the creation of the world (Gen. 2:2) and was still operable at the time of the wilderness wanderings (Ps. 95:7-11). The author's logic follows that the word σήμερον (Ps. 95:7c), spoken through David years after the wilderness event, means the promise of rest still stands (Heb. 4:7). Those who failed to enter the rest, falling in the wilderness, failed because of their disobedience (Heb. 4:6,11). Therefore, those who now enter the promised rest will enter by faithful obedience.

Warning: Consider the Power of God's Word
(Heb. 4:12-13)

Heb. 4:12-13 offers another warning for the community. Here the author depicts the word of God as an active force of judgement from

---

[40] Supra, 66.
[41] Supra, 67-68.

which no one may hide. As Harold Attridge notes, the warning probably refers to the divine word mentioned in the quotes from Ps. 95 (Heb. 3:7-11,15; 4:3, 7).[42] Just as the promise of rest still stands, so does the "oath" of anger and judgement for those who follow the example of disobedience provided by those who fell in the wilderness.

The Present Problem with the Community
(Heb. 5:11-6:3)

At Heb. 5:11-6:3 the author of Hebrews, for the first time in the discourse, explicitly cites the critical problem with his hearers—they are sluggish learners who need to move on to spiritual maturity. They need a refresher course in elementary tenets of the Christian faith (i.e., repentance from sin, faith in God, etc. in Heb. 6:1-3). The solution is to move on to maturity (6:1).

Warning: The Danger of Falling Away
from the Christian Faith
(Heb. 6:4-8)

The harsh warning found in Heb. 6:4-8 speaks concerning the fate awaiting those who, having experienced the Christian faith, fall away from that faith. Where else can they go for repentance? They are rejecting the only One who can effect true forgiveness of sins. The agricultural analogy reinforces the negative message. Destruction lies in the path of those who like unresponsive crops fail to produce good fruit.

Mitigation: The Author's Confidence in
and Desire for the Hearers
(Heb. 6:9-12)

The author, however, has great confidence in his audience. He expects they will experience the better things that naturally accompany salvation. Their past works show that they love God and His people. What they need now is to overcome their laziness through diligence, which may be had in part by imitating those who through faith and patience inherit the promises.

---

[42] Attridge, *The Epistle to the Hebrews*, 133.

Warning: The Danger of Rejecting
God's Truth and God's Son
(Heb. 10:26-31)

A fourth warning, and the second warning to use an *a fortiori* argument, occurs at Heb. 10:26-32. Once again the primary elements are the rejection of God's truth and the consequences of that rejection. Here those who continue to sin, rejecting God's Son, have no expectation of forgiveness but only of judgement. No sacrifice for sins remains. The author has already shown the old covenant system to be inferior, and they persist in turning away from the One offering the superior new covenant sacrifice. If those who rejected the law of Moses were punished without mercy, certainly those who reject the Son will experience the dread of "falling into the hands of the living God."

The Positive Example of the Hearers' Past and an Admonition
to Endure to Receive the Promise
(Heb. 10:32-39)

The community being addressed has numerous examples of those who have endured in the past—including themselves. The preacher reminds them of their strength amidst past suffering. They had been insulted and persecuted and had shared the burden with others of like experience. He exhorts them to build on that past experience and persevere to the reception of their reward. To have done the will of God in the past is not enough. Those who do the will of God and endure in the doing of it are the ones to receive the promise.

The Positive Example of the Old Testament Faithful
(Heb. 11:1-40)

The example list of Hebrews 11 functions to provide the audience with overwhelming evidence that along the path of faith (and, therefore, faithful endurance) lies commendation.[43] The positive example of the Old Testament faithful confronts the listeners with the absurdity of following any other course. Furthermore, they endured even though they (like the hearers themselves [10:36]) had not yet received what had been promised.

---

[43] Cosby, "The Rhetorical Composition of Hebrews 11," 268.

Reject Sin and Fix Your Eyes on Jesus,
Supreme Example of Endurance
(Heb. 12:1-2)

What then should be the Christian's response to the overwhelming evidence provided by the Old Testament men and women of faith? The exhortation at Heb. 12:1-2 is two-fold. First, the believer should jettison the sin which keeps him from effective running. Second, he should look to Jesus, the successful race-runner who endured, scoffed at the shame he experienced, and now sits at the right hand of God. Jesus provides the greatest example of faithful endurance, an example both living and present and one on whom the hearers should fix their eyes.

Endure Discipline as Sons
(Heb. 12:3-17)

With Heb. 12:3-17 the discourse returns to the topic of the hearers' sonship for the first time since 2:10-18. The unit begins with a transitional admonition to consider Jesus who endured extreme opposition from wicked men.[44] The author points out that the hearers have yet to shed blood in the struggle (as Jesus had on the cross) and should look to Jesus' example so that they might endure.

As further encouragement the preacher presents a short midrashic treatment of Prov. 3:11-12. Picking up on the references to Υἱέ, παιδείας, and κύριος he explains that discipline is a normal aspect of the father-son relationship. In fact, discipline is a sign of legitimate sonship. He argues *a fortiori* that if the hearers respected their earthly disciplinarians, they certainly should respect their spiritual Father, submitting to him in the midst of discipline. Earthly fathers discipline out of a limited perspective, but God disciplines for the good of his sons, that they might be holy.

Heb. 12:12-17 continues the theme of holiness. The strengthening of weak arms and knees relates to staying on the path of right living, as the reference to Prov. 4:26 (12:13) demonstrates. The author goes on to exhort the hearers to live holy lives and ends the section

---

[44] The transition is effected by the hook word relationship between the two forms of ὑπομένω (vv. 2, 3). The two units are also linked by the semantic relationship between ἀφορῶντες (v. 2) and ἀναλογίσασθε (v. 3) and between σταυρὸν (v. 2) and ὑπὸ τῶν ἁμαρτωλῶν εἰς ἑαυτὸν (v. 3).

with the negative example of Esau. As an unholy son Esau rejected his inheritance and, therefore, experienced rejection. The Christian community must not follow Esau's example by choosing the path of sin over the promised inheritance.

The Blessings of the New Covenant
(Heb. 12:18-24)

The highly stylized periodic sentence running from 12:18-24 consists of rhythmic phrases detailing the horrors of Mt. Sinai set over against the joys of Zion. The emphatically placed Οὐ (12:18) which begins the unit finds its balance in the ἀλλά of verse 22. The author offers strong encouragement for his hearers, demonstrating how their orientation is distinctly different from those who fell in the wilderness. The wilderness wanderers standing before Sinai faced the dreadful sights (burning fire, darkness, gloom, storm) and sounds (the trumpet blast and the voice) of God's strict judgement (v. 20). The hearers, however, have come to a different mountain, Mt. Zion. They have a citizenship in the heavenly Jerusalem and fellowship with thousands of celebrating angels, members of the church on earth (v. 23a), and those who have already died (v. 23c). Especially, they have come to Jesus, the mediator of a new covenant. Jesus' blood speaks better than the blood of Abel, whose blood cried out for judgement. By contrast, Jesus' blood proclaims the penalty paid in full.

Warning: Do Not Reject God's Word
(Heb. 12:25-29)

The fifth and final warning is found at Heb. 12:25-29. As in the warnings of 2:1-4 and 10:26-31 the preacher uses an *a fortiori* argument. If those who rejected the voice from Mt. Sinai did not escape, then those who turn away from the heavenly warning certainly will not escape. The earth shook at Sinai but that shaking will pale in comparison to the shaking promised in Haggai 2:6. The author interprets the Haggai passage to mean that the created order will be done away with—the coming judgement of God will shake the cosmos, crumbling its very foundation. Therefore, the hearers should worship God reverently and give Him thanks for their part in the unshakable kingdom.

Concluding Practical Exhortations (Heb. 13:1-19), Benediction (Heb. 13:20-21), and Closing (Heb. 13:22-25)

A number of critics have questioned the integrity of chapter thirteen on the bases of abruptness, form, and content. However, these concerns have been soundly answered by drawing attention to vocabulary, uses of the Old Testament, conceptual ties with the rest of the book, patterns of argumentation, structural patterns, and literary style, all of which witness to the homogeneity of the chapter with the previous twelve chapters. Due to the strength of studies affirming chapter thirteen's integrity, the burden of proof has fallen to the skeptics.[45]

The author concludes the previous unit with an admonition for the hearers to live out worshipful service to God. Heb. 13:1-19 spells out practical guidelines for serving God. The section falls into two sub-sections. The first six verses provide general paraenesis which would have been familiar throughout the Christian churches. Heb. 13:7-19 concerns the community's relationship with leaders, guarding against heresy, suffering for Christ, true Christian sacrifices, and prayer for the author.

The benediction of Heb. 13:20-21 probably was the ending to the original sermon, and the closing, found in verses 22-25, an addendum added when the manuscript was sent by courier.[46]

BROADER DYNAMICS OF COHESION
WITHIN THE HORTATORY UNITS

When these hortatory units are considered for the cohesive dynamics by which they relate, several observations may be made.

---

[45] For a helpful summary of the discussion see William L. Lane, *Hebrews 9-13*, Word Biblical Commentary (Dallas: Word, 1991), 495-507. For arguments in favor of the chapter's integrity with the rest of Hebrews see especially Lane (mentioned above), Floyd V. Filson, *'Yesterday': A Study of Hebrews in Light of Chapter 13*, Studies in Biblical Theology (Naperville, IL: Alec R. Allenson, 1967); C. R. Williams, "A Word-Study of Hebrews 13," *Journal of Biblical Literature* 30 (1911): 129-36; R. V. G. Tasker, "The Integrity of the Epistle to the Hebrews," *Expository Times* 47 (1935-36): 136-38; Albert Vanhoye, "La question littéraire de Hébreux xiii.1-6," *New Testament Studies* 23 (1976-77): 121-39.

[46] So Lane, *Hebrews 9-13*, 497.

Parallels Between the Warning Passages

First, there are striking parallels between the five warning passages located at 2:1-4, 4:12-13, 6:4-8, 10:26-31, and 12:25-29. Each of these warnings concerns the hearers' relationship to the word of God and the judgement of God. All but 4:12-13 speak expressly concerning the rejection of that word. Especially prominent are the parallels between the three warnings built around *a fortiori* arguments (2:1-4, 10:26-31, and 12:25-29). In each of these the rejection of the law of Moses is the "lesser" situation and the rejection of God's word to the hearers (salvation in 2:3; the truth in 10:26; the warning from heaven in 12:25) the greater situation. In each the author makes the point that those who reject God's word face severe punishment.

Groupings of Hortatory Units

Second, the other hortatory units may grouped in four main sections. Those running from 3:1-4:11 deal with faithfulness. Heb. 3:1-6 presents Jesus as the supreme example of a faithful son. The author sets forth a graphic example of faithlessness and the cost of faithlessness in Heb. 3:7-19. Finally, the hearers' opportunity for the reward of "rest," which comes by obedience, finds expression in Heb. 4:3-11.

The two units which flank the warning at 6:4-8 form another group and confront the hearers' present problem. Heb. 5:11-6:3 details the problem and 6:9-12 then softens the harsh warning of verses 4-8 with mitigation.

Five units are located at Heb. 10:32-12:24. These are 10:32-39, 11:1-40, 12:1-2, 12:3-17, and 12:18-24. All but the last of these deal with endurance. The positive example of the hearers' past endurance is the topic of Heb. 10:32-39. The example list of Hebrews 11 provides the hearers with numerous positive examples of heros of the Old Testament who endured by faith. Jesus, the supreme example of endurance, is the topic of Heb. 12:1-2, and in Heb. 12:3-17 the author exhorts the community to endure discipline as true sons. The unit at 12:18-24 concerns the blessings of the new covenant. Its unique role in the discourse will be dealt with below.

The final group consists of the practical exhortations, the benediction, and the closing in chapter 13. Warning passages bracket the first and third of these groups. The second group has the warning in the middle.

Distant Parallels in Addition to Those Noted Among the Warning Passages
Third, in addition to the parallel relationships marked among the
warning passages in Hebrews, distant parallelism may be recognized between other pairs of hortatory units in the discourse. "Jesus,
the Supreme Example of a Faithful Son" (3:1-6) mirrors "Reject
Sin and Fix Your Eyes on Jesus, Supreme Example of Endurance"
(12:1-2). In both passages the hearers are exhorted to look to Jesus
as an example. The midrash on the Old Testament unfaithful who
fell in the wilderness (3:7-19) finds its balance in the *exempla* of
chapter 11. Also, in Heb. 4:3-11 the hearers are presented with the
present promise of "rest" for those of faith who are obedient to God.
The passage parallels Heb. 10:32-39 in which the hearers are reminded of the positive example of their own past faithfulness and
exhorted to endure to receive the promise. Finally, the author's
statement concerning the community's present problem in 5:11-6:3
is nicely complemented by his mitigation of 6:9-12.

Based on the relationships observed between these hortatory units, the warning passages, and the overlapping transitions at 4:14-16
and 10:19-25, the units running from 3:1-12:2 may be laid out in an
elaborate chiasmus, as seen in fig. 31.[47] Note that the hortatory
elements of the overlapping transitions are inverted in the text.

3:1-6 Jesus, the Supreme Example of a Faithful Son
   3:7-19 The Negative Example of Those Who Fell through
      Faithlessness
      4:3-11 The Promise of Rest for Those Who are Faithful
         4:12-13 *WARNING*
            4:14-16 Hold Fast and Draw Near
               5:11-6:3 The Present Problem with the Hearers
                  6:4-8 *WARNING*
               6:9-12 Mitigation: The Author's Confidence in and Desire
                  for the Hearers
            0:19-25 Draw Near and Hold Fast
         10:26-31 *WARNING*
      10:32-39 The Positive Example of the Hearers' Past and an
         Admonition to Endure to Receive the Promise
   11:1-40 The Positive Example of the Old Testament Faithful
12:1-2 Reject Sin and Fix Your Eyes on Jesus, Supreme Example of
   Endurance

Fig. 31. The chiastic structure of hortatory units in Hebrews from Heb. 3:1-12:2.

---

[47] Intermediary transitions are not included in the chiastic structure.

Reiteration of Key Themes
Woven through the hortatory units are key themes around which the hortatory program coheres. As seen in fig. 32, these themes are "rebel/drift/fall away," "sin/sinfulness," "punishment/judgement," "promise/reward/inheritance," "receive," "word of God/message," "speak," "God," "Jesus/Son," "faith/believe," "faithfulness/ obedience," "endure," "enter/go on/approach," and "example." Whereas the expositional material focuses on major themes section by section (e.g., "angels" in 1:1-2:18, "Melchizedek" in 7:1-28, "offering" in 8:3-10:18, etc.), the hortatory material returns again and again to these focal motifs. These motifs are set in various contexts of warning, encouragement, and both positive and negative examples.

Through his hortatory constituents the author sets forth a dichotomy of decision for the community. Fig. 33 offers a paradigm depicting this dichotomy.

The preacher asserts that God has spoken his eschatological word to his people and that it is either a word of promise or a word of punishment.[48] The promise of inheritance may be gained by endurance through faith. Those who do not endure, rebelling against God, fall back to destruction.[49] In order to spur his hearers on to a right decision the author gives both positive and negative examples,[50] both encouragement and warning.[51]

---

[48] Promise: 3:6; 4:3-11; 6:13-20; 10:35-36; 12:22-24. Punishment: 2:1-4; 3:7-11; 4:1-2,12-13;6:7-8; 10:26-31,38; 12:14-17,18-21,25-29. On the community's relationship to the word of God see Käsemann, *The Wandering People of God*, 17-18.

[49] Endure: 4:3,11,14-15; 6:12; 10:23,32-36,39; 11:2-12:2. Fall back: 2:1; 3:12-4:2; 6:4-6; 10:37-38. Therefore, the spatial motion in the hortatory material is "horizontal" rather than "vertical" between heaven and earth. The exception is Heb. 12:1-2,18-29.

[50] Positive examples: Jesus (3:1-6; 12:1-2) in comparison with Moses (3:1-6); Abraham (6:13-15); the hearers' past success (10:32-34); the heroes of faith (11:2-40). Negative examples: the wilderness wanderers (3:7-4:2); Christians contemporary with the hearers who have fallen away (6:4-6); Esau (12:15-17).

On the use of examples in ancient rhetoric see Watson, *Invention, Arrangement, and Style*, 16. On the use of examples in hellenistic synagogue sermons see Thyen, *Der Stil des jüdisch-hellenistischen Homilie*, 13, 18, 30, 75-76. Also see Cosby, "The Rhetorical Composition of Hebrews 11," 250-70.

[51] Encouragement: 3:1,12-13; 6:1-3,9-12; 10:32-34; 12:4-13,18-24. Warning: 2:1-4; 4:12-13; 6:7-8; 10:26-31; 12:25-29.

	2:1-4	3:1-6	3:7-19	4:3-11	4:12-13	4:14-16	5:11-6:3	6:4-8	6:9-12	10:19-25	10:26-31	10:32-39	11:1-40	12:1-2	12:3-17	12:18-24	12:25-29	13:1-19
rebel/fall away/drift	X		X	X				X				X			X		X	
sin/sinfulness		X	X			X	X	X			X	X	X	X	X		X	
punishment/judgement	X	X	X	X	X	X	X	X			X	X			X	X	X	
promise/reward/inheritance	X	X	X						X	X		X	X		X		X	
example		X	X				X	X			X	X	X	X	X		X	X
word of God/message	X	X	X	X		X	X	X			X	X	X		X		X	X
speak	X	X	X			X	X	X			X					X	X	
God	X	X	X	X	X	X	X	X	X	X	X	X	X	X	X	X	X	X
Jesus/Son/H.P.	X	X	X	X	X	X			X	X		X	X	X	X	X	X	X
faith/believe		X				X	X		X	X		X	X	X				X
faithfulness/obedience		X	X		X					X		X	X				X	X
endure		X	X						X	X		X	X	X	X			
enter/go on/approach	X	X	X	X	X	X	X		X	X		X	X	X	X	X	X	X

Fig. 32. Key themes in the hortatory material of Hebrews.

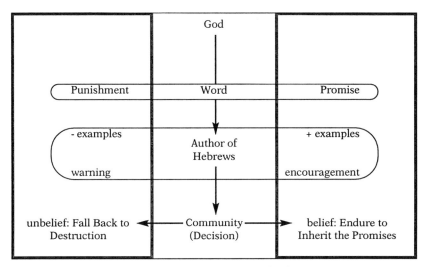

Fig. 33. The hortatory message of Hebrews.

The Function of Hortatory Units in Hebrews

Through the reiteration of central motifs—by encouraging words, warnings, and examples—the author hammers home repeatedly the reward of a right decision on the part of the community and the punishment awaiting those who make a bad decision. The primary function of the hortatory material is emotional rather than educational. Here he does not merely seek to build the hearers' knowledge of a particular topic. Rather, he attempts to challenge his hearers to right action, eliciting an emotional response from them. This purpose behind the author's uses of exhortation may be set in contrast to his expositional teaching concerning the Son. The two genres, however, work well together in execution of the overall semantic program behind the macro-discourse.

HOW THE TWO GENRES WORK TOGETHER IN THE STRUCTURE OF HEBREWS

A number of structural connections tying the expository to the hortatory units in Hebrews have been noted in the study thus far. In addition to hook words, the overlapping constituent transitions at

Heb. 4:14-16 and 10:19-25 and the ingressive intermediary transition at 6:13-20 bring the two genres together structurally.[52]

In addition to these structural links, broader semantic associations weave the two genres in the development of the discourse.
These associations may be demonstrated in terms of "semantic borrowing" and "semantic overlap." The nature of these relationships
directly addresses an important question in the structure-of-He-
brews debate: Does the author use the expositional material to serve
the hortatory or the hortatory as a stylistic digression from the expositional?

Semantic Borrowing

In every instance in Hebrews where expositional material is followed by hortatory, the hortatory utilizes semantic material from
the expositional discussion. Graham Hughes, in his work *Hebrews
and Hermeneutics: The Epistle to the Hebrews as a New Testament Example
of Biblical Interpretation*, has clearly demonstrated the rhetorical relationship between Heb. 1:5-14 and Heb. 2:1-4.[53] The "Son Superior
to the Angels" motif (1:5-14) lays the foundation for the *a fortiori*
argument of 2:1-4. By the end of the chain quotation in the first
chapter the hearers are shaking their heads in agreement that the
Son is indeed superior to the angels. The preacher then turns to
address the community directly, hitting them with the argument
from lesser to greater: "If rejection of the word delivered through
angels deserved punishment, how much more does rejection of the
word delivered through the Son deserve punishment?" The exhortation "borrows" semantic material from the exposition to accomplish its purpose.

The relationship between Heb. 2:10-18 and the hortatory material which follows is more subtle. Within Heb. 2:10-18 the author
addresses the hearers' "sonship" in the context of the Son's incarnation. Heb. 3:1-6 follows with discussion of Jesus' faithfulness as Son.
Those just addressed as "sons" are exhorted to follow the example
of "sonship faithfulness" provided by the Son. Thus the topic of

---

[52] Supra, 102-103, 110-11.

[53] Graham Hughes, *Hebrews and Hermeneutics: The Epistle to the Hebrews as a New
Testament Example of Biblical Interpretation* (Cambridge: Cambridge University
Press, 1979), 7-9.

faithfulness (3:1-4:11) relates to the topic of sonship raised initially in Heb. 2:10-18.

The semantic relationship between Heb. 5:1-10 and the hortatory digression of Heb. 5:11-6:20 is effected through the ingressive intermediary transition at 6:13-20. The abrupt interruption of the exposition at 5:11 serves to grab the hearers' attention and focus it on the present problem with the community (5:11-6:3). As detailed in the discussion on transitions, Heb. 6:13-20 accesses semantic material from Heb. 5:1-10 in order to move to the discussion of Melchizedek and Jesus' Melchizedekan priesthood (7:1-28).[54]

Numerous elements from the expositional material are utilized in the massive, rolling exhortation of 10:26-13:21. In addition to the overlapping transition at Heb. 10:19-25, the author uses *gezerah shawah* to move from the embedded discourse concerning the superior offering (8:3-10:18) to the hortatory material which follows. The *Stichworten* ἤχω and εὐδόκησας from Ps. 40:6-7 (Heb. 10:6-7) are echoed with ὁ ἐρχόμενος ἥξει and εὐδοκεῖ from Hab. 2:3-4 (Heb. 10:37-38).[55] The warning at Heb. 10:26-31 includes references to the sacrifice for sins (10:26) and the blood of the covenant (10:29). Heb. 12:1-2 refers to the cross and contains the only allusion to Ps. 110:1 outside the expositional material. Semantic borrowing from the expositional material is especially noted at Heb. 12:18-24. Here are found references to angels (12:22), heaven (12:22-23), the spirits of righteous men (12:23), Jesus' mediation of the new covenant (12:24), and to his sprinkled blood (12:24). The practical exhortations and benediction of Heb. 13:1-21 conclude the discourse with references to the expositional discussion, including mention of angels (13:2), the constancy of Christ's nature (13:8), the altar, tabernacle and sacrifices (13:10-15), resurrection from the dead (13:20), and a final reference to the blood of the covenant (13:20). Therefore, in varying degrees the hortatory material builds on elements from the expositional material.

Semantic Overlap

As demonstrated in Chapter 6 of this study, the most important lexical and pronominal elements which serve to unify the whole of

---

[54] Supra, 110-11.
[55] Ellis, *The Old Testament in Early Christianity*, 107.

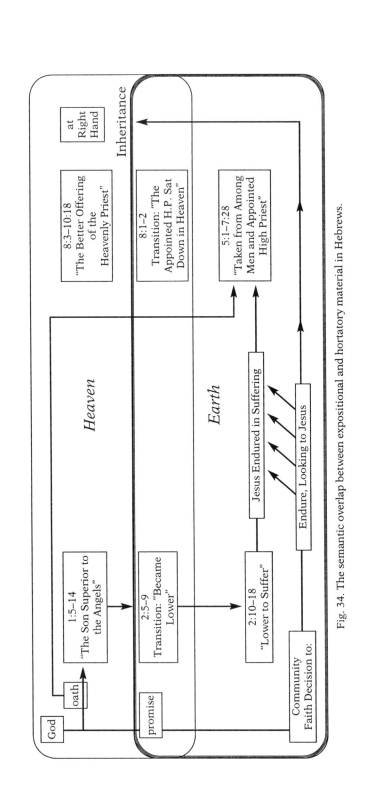

Fig. 34. The semantic overlap between expositional and hortatory material in Hebrews.

Hebrews are (1) the word θεός, flanked by pronominal references to God, (2) various lexical items used as designations for God's Son, along with pronominals used in conjunction with those designations, (3) terms related to "the word of God," and (4) pronominal references to the members of the Christian community being addressed.[56] These lexical and pronominal elements display a semantic overlap between the two genres and point to the purpose of the author's discourse.

Simply put, the purpose of the book of Hebrews is to exhort the hearers to endure in their pursuit of the promised reward, in obedience to the word of God, and especially on the basis of their new covenant relationship with the Son. The overlap between the expositional and hortatory material in the book lies in the relationship of the community to whom God has spoken his word, with the Son, of whom and to whom God has also spoken. In the expositional units the discourse deals with information about the Son. In the hortatory units the author turns to his hearers and exhorts them to take action. It is especially on the basis of the hearers' relationship with the Son that they have a superior basis for taking the desired action. This semantic overlap between the expositional and hortatory material is depicted in fig. 34.

This integrated message of the macro-discourse is most clearly seen at Heb. 3:1-6 and 12:1-2, the overlapping transitions at 4:14-16 and 10:19-25, the ingressive intermediary transition of 6:13-20, and 12:18-24, which may be considered the climax of the discourse. The hearers should "hold fast" and "draw near" because they have a great high priest who has passed through the heavens and leads them there (4:14-16; 10:19-25). They should look to Jesus, the high priest who has established the new covenant (12:24) by entering the veil (6:19-20; 10:19-20) as their supreme hope (6:19-20) and example of endurance (3:1-6; 12:1-2). The discourse is brought to a climax at 12:18-24 with the stylistic contrast between the hearers and those who fell in the wilderness. Here the supreme basis for endurance is stated in no uncertain terms. The hearers are under the new covenant established by Christ's sacrifice.

Therefore, the expositional material serves the hortatory purpose of the whole work. The exposition on Christ's position in relation to

---

[56] Supra, 90-92.

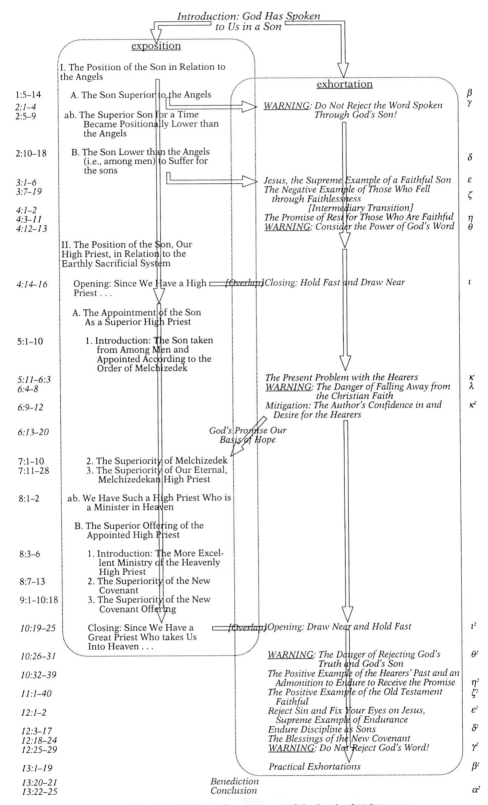

Fig. 35. A structural assessment of the book of Hebrews.

the angels and his position as the superior high priest does more than theologically inform; it offers a powerful motivation for active obedience and endurance in the race toward the lasting city.

How Should Hebrews be Outlined?

How, then, can the orchestration of structural dynamics in Hebrews be depicted so as to best reflect the unique functions of each of the main genres in the book? The approach set forth in fig. 35 depicts development of the expositional units with "outline form" (i.e., IA, IB, etc.) based on the outline presented in fig. 28 (supra, 117). This reflects the logical, point-by-point argument executed in the expositional material.

The hortatory units, on the other hand, rather than being forced under the expositional outline, are set apart in the column to the right and allowed to relate to other units to which they seem to correspond. This scheme may not make for an attractive outline, but it serves to highlight the functions of the individual units within the broader discourse.

Placed in this manner, the units before Heb. 3:1-6 (even those which are expositional) and after 12:1-2 may be seen as also participating in a chiastic structure. In the discourse, believers are only referred to as "sons" at 2:10-18 and 12:3-17.[57] If the intermediary transition of 2:5-9 and the climax of 12:18-24 are bracketed, the warning of 2:1-4 clearly finds its parallel in the warning of 12:25-29.

The correspondence between Heb. 1:5-14 and the practical exhortation of Hebrews 13 is not obvious. However, the exposition of 1:5-14 leads into the warning of 2:1-4, and the warning of 12:25-29 gives rise to the practical exhortation of 13:1-19. This scheme puts the introduction to the book (1:1-4) in balance with the benediction (13:20-21).

Furthermore, the expositional material from Heb. 5:1 through 10:18 need not be forced into the chiasmus since the correspondences within that major expositional block have already been demonstrated.[58]

---

[57] The reference to Esau (12:14-17) finds expression because of his rejection of his birthright. He did not value his sonship. Thus the Esau pericope relates to the concept of sonship expounded previously in Hebrews 12.

[58] Supra, 119-21.

If the chiastic structure depicted in fig. 35 is an accurate assessment of the book's organization, then it would mean that there are two points which may be considered "center points" in the development of the discourse. The warning at Heb. 6:4-8 would be the center point for the hortatory material, the author utilizing that digression effectively to gain the hearers' attention. The intermediary transition at Heb. 8:1-2 could be considered the center point for the great central exposition on the high priestly ministry of Christ. It may be suggested that the concept of the two genres moving in concert, but not exact correspondence, makes sense. They move along different lines but hasten toward the same goal. Each in its own way builds toward the goal of challenging the hearers to endure. The expositional material builds toward the goal by focusing on the appointed high priest as a superior basis for endurance. The hortatory passages move toward the goal by reiteration of warnings, promises, and examples used to challenge the hearers to endure.

CONCLUSIONS

The problems caused by the complex structure of Hebrews are not easily answered; they may never be answered with a consensus of New Testament scholarship. Hopefully, discussions on the book's structure will continue and further insights will move us toward clarification of the discourse.

Perhaps part of the difficulty with depicting Hebrews in outline form lies in the fact that Hebrews was originally delivered for its effect on hearers.[59] The discourse was not crafted to fit our neat, thematically progressing outlines. It was meant to have an impact on listeners. The switch back and forth between a logically developing exposition and a challenging exhortation would have been highly effective. For the author to give an introduction to the appointment of the Son as high priest (5:1-10) and then suddenly to break off and confront the hearers directly with their immediate problem (5:11-6:3) may do damage to our outlines, but it would have made a rhetorical impact. As Chrysostom suggested long ago, the ears of the listeners would have been turned vigorously toward the speaker by the time he resumed his discussion of Melchizedek at Heb. 7:1.[60]

---

[59] In this regard see Lindars, "The Rhetorical Structure of Hebrews," 382-406.
[60] Chrysostom, "ΟΜΙΛΙΑ ΙΒ΄," 423.

Second, the agnostic position on the structure of Hebrews is unnecessary, since relations between units in the discourse can be clearly demonstrated. The exposition in Hebrews is much easier to track through the discourse because of the nature of its development. Yet, if the author is allowed his own conventions, the distant parallelism between hortatory units in Hebrews may also provide insight into the structure.

Third, transition devices and inclusions must be taken into consideration in studies regarding the book's organization. The transitions in Hebrews especially confuse the development in the discourse if the principles behind them are not understood. The uses of *gezerah shawah* and *a fortiori* argumentation have also served to highlight the need to understand rabbinic methods of interpretation as employed by the author.

Analysis of cohesion shifts demands more consideration as a potentially helpful method in working through the structure of biblical literature. The method certainly will need refining, but it does provide an objective means of analysis that moves assessment of unit boundaries beyond subjective decisions.

One question that will be asked is, "Did the original hearers discern and understand all the devices used in Hebrews?" Two suggestions are plausible and are offered in closing.

First, as children of their day they probably would have been familiar with devices such as *inclusio, haraz,* and *gezerah shawah*. The fact that these techniques are used so extensively in Hebrews is, obviously, a witness to their use in the first century.

Second, however, the hearers would not have had to catch every twist and turn in the discourse for the discourse to have had a great *effect on them*. As an analogy, I enjoy the music of Mozart. I do not read a note of music and certainly do not understand how the great composer brings all the various themes together in such powerful performances; but I do not have to in order to recognize them as powerful. I can be moved even in my ignorance. The author of Hebrews was a highly skilled individual, a "Mozart" of oratory, and his discourse a "symphony" of form. His message still moves those who truly hear the word of exhortation.

BIBLIOGRAPHY

Commentaries

Aquinas, Thomas. *In Omnes S. Pauli Apostoli Epistolas Commentaria*. Taurini: Petri Marietti, 1924.

Attridge, Harold. *To the Hebrews*. Hermeneia. Philadelphia, PA: Fortress Press, 1989.

Betz, Hans-Dieter. *Galatians: A Commentary of Paul's Letter to the Churches in Galatia*. Hermeneia. Philadelphia, PA: Fortress Press, 1979.

———. *2 Corinthians 8 and 9: A Commentary on Two Administrative Letters of the Apostle Paul*. Hermeneia. Philadelphia, PA: Fortress Press, 1985.

Bruce, F. F. *The Epistle to the Hebrews*. New International Commentary on the New Testament. Grand Rapids: Eerdmans, 1964.

Bourke, Myles M. *The Epistle to the Hebrews*. Englewood Cliffs, NJ: Printice Hall, 1990.

Buchanan, George W. *To the Hebrews*. The Anchor Bible. Garden City, NY: Doubleday & Co., 1972.

Bullinger, Heinrich. *In Piam et Eruditam Pauli ad Hebraeos Epistolam, Heinrychi Bullingeri Commentarius*. Zürich: Christoph Froschouer, 1532.

Calvin, John. *Commentaries on the Epistle to the Hebrews*. Translated by John Owen. Grand Rapids, MI: Wm. B. Eerdmans, 1949.

Delitzsch, Franz. *Commentary on the Epistle to the Hebrews*. Translated by Thomas L. Kingsbury. Grand Rapids, MI: Wm. B. Eerdmans, 1952.

Dibelius, Martin. *James: A Commentary on the Epistle of James*. Translated by Michael A. Williams. Hermeneia. Philadelphia, PA: Fortress Press, 1976.

Ebrard, John H. A. *Biblical Commentary on the Epistle to the Hebrews*. Clark's Foreign Theological Library. Translated by John Fulton. Edinburgh: T. & T. Clark, 1853.

Hagner, Donald A. *Hebrews*. New International Biblical Commentary. Peabody, MA: Hendrickson, 1990.

Hemmingsen, Niels. *Commentaria in omnes Epistolas Apostolorum, Pauli, Petri, Iudae, Ioannis, Iacobi, et in eam quae ad Hebraeos inscribitur*. Frankfurt: Georg Corvinus, 1579.

Héring, Jean. *L'Épître aux Hébreux*. Commentaire du Nouveau Testament. Paris: Delachaux & Niestlé, 1954.

Hillmann, Willibrord. *Der Brief an die Hebräer*. Edited by Josef Hillmann. Düsseldorf: Patmos-Verlag, 1965.

Hughes, P. E. *A Commentary on the Epistle to the Hebrews*. Grand Rapids, MI: William B. Eerdmans, 1977.

Kistemaker, Simon J. *Exposition of the Epistle to the Hebrews*. New Testament Commentary. Grand Rapids, MI: Baker Book House, 1984.

Lane, William L. *Hebrews 1-8*. Word Biblical Commentary. Dallas, TX: Word, 1991.

———. *Hebrews 9-13*. Word Biblical Commentary. Dallas, TX: Word, 1991.

Lenski, R. C. H. *The Interpretation of the Epistle to the Hebrews and the Epistle of James*. Minneapolis, MN: Augsburg Publishing House, 1966.

Lünemann, Gottlieb. *Critical and Exegetical Handbook to the Epistle to the Hebrews*. Critical and Exegetical Commentary on the New Testament. Translated by Maurice J. Evans. Edinburgh: T. & T. Clark, 1882.

Michel, Otto. *Der Brief an die Hebräer.* Kritisch-exegetischer Kommentar über das Neue Testament. Göttingen: Vandenhoeck & Ruprecht, 1966.

Moffatt, James. *A Critical and Exegetical Commentary on the Epistle to the Hebrews.* The International Critical Commentary. New York: Charles Scribner's Sons, 1924.

Moll, Carl Bernhard. *The Epistle to the Hebrews.* Translated by Philip Schaff. Commentary on the Holy Scriptures. New York: Charles Scribner's Sons, 1887.

Montefiore, Hugh. *A Commentary on the Epistle to the Hebrews.* Black's New Testament Commentaries. London: Adam & Charles Black, 1964.

Nairne, Alexander. *Epistle of Priesthood: Studies in the Epistle to the Hebrews.* Edinburgh: T. & T. Clark, 1913.

Owen, John. *Hebrews: The Epistle of Warning.* Grand Rapids, MI: Kregel Publications, 1968.

Rendall, Frederic. *The Epistle to the Hebrews.* London: MacMillan and Co., 1888.

Riggenbach, D. Eduard. *Der Brief an die Hebräer.* Kommentar zum Neuen Testament. Leipzig: A. Deichert, 1913.

Spicq, Ceslas. *L'Épitre aux Hébreux.* 2 vols. Paris: Gabalda, 1952-53.

———. *L'Épître aux Hébreux.* Sources Bibliques. Paris: J. Gabalda, 1977.

Stuart, Moses. *A Commentary on the Epistle to the Hebrews.* Reprint. London: Fisher, Son, & Co., 1833.

Theodoret. "Commentarius in omnes sancti Pauli Epistolas." Patrologia Graeca. Paris: J.-P. Migne, 1862.

Von Soden, Hermann Frhr. *Hebräerbrief, Briefe des Petrus, Jakobus, Judas.* 3d ed. Hand-Commentar zum Neue Testament. Tübingen: J. C. B. Mohr (Paul Siebeck), 1899.

Weiss, Bernhard. *Kristisch Exegetisches Handbuch über den Brief an die Hebräer.* Kritisch Exegetischer Kommentar über das Neue Testament. Göttingen: Vandenhoeck und Ruprecht's, 1888.

Westcott, Brooke Foss. *The Epistle to the Hebrews: The Greek Text with Notes and Essays.* London: MacMillan and Co., 1929.

Wilson, R. M. *Hebrews.* New Century Bible Commentary. Grand Rapids, MI: Wm. B. Eerdmans, 1987.

Windisch, Hans. *Der Hebräerbrief.* Handbuch zum Neuen Testament. Tübingen: J. C. B. Mohr (Paul Siebeck), 1931.

Zwingli, H. *In evangelicam historicam de domino nostro Iesu Christo, per Matthaeum, Marcum, Lucam, et Joannem conscriptam, epistolasque aliquot Pauli, annotationes D. Huldrychi Zwinglii per Leonem Iudae exceptae et aeditae. Adjecta est epistola Pauli ad Hebraeos, et Joannis Apostoli epistola per Gasparem Megandrum.* Zürich: Christoph Froschouer, 1539.

Miscellaneous Works

Atkins, J. W. H. *Literary Criticism in Antiquity: A Sketch of its Development.* Gloucester, MA: Peter Smith, 1961.

Aune, David E. *The New Testament in its Literary Environment.* Library of Early Christianity. Philadelphia, PA: Westminster Press, 1987.

Ball, Ivan Jay. *A Rhetorical Study of Zephaniah.* Berkeley, CA: BIBAL Press, 1988.

Barrett, C. K. "The Eschatology of the Epistle to the Hebrews." In *Background of the New Testament and Its Eschatology,* ed. W. D. Davies and D. Daube, 363-93. Cambridge: University Press, 1956.

Barth, Markus. "The Old Testament in Hebrews." In *Issues in New Testament Interpretation,* ed. W. Klassen and G. F. Snyder, 65-78. New York: Harper and Row, 1962.

Bengel, John Albert. *Gnomon of the New Testament*. Translated by James Bryce. 6th ed. Edinburgh: T. & T. Clark, 1866.

Berger, Klaus. *Exegese des Neuen Testaments: Neue Wege vom Text zur Auslegung*. 2d ed. Heidelberg: Quelle & Meyer, 1984.

Black, David Allen. *Linguistics, Biblical Semantics, and Bible Translation: An Annotated Bibliography of Periodical Literature from 1961*. La Mirada, CA: Biola University, 1984.

——. *Linguistics for Students of New Testament Greek: A Survey of Basic Concepts and Applications*. Grand Rapids, MI: Baker Book House, 1988.

Blass, F., and A. Debrunner. *A Greek Grammar of the New Testament and Other Early Christian Literature*. Translated by Robert W. Funk. Chicago: University of Chicago Press, 1961.

Borgen, Peder. *Bread From Heaven: An Exegetical Study of the Concept of Manna in the Gospel of John and the Writings of Philo*. Supplements to Novum Testamentum. Leiden: E. J. Brill, 1965.

Bowker, John. *The Targums and Rabbinic Literature: An Introduction to Jewish Interpretation of Scripture*. Cambridge: The University Press, 1969.

Bruce, F. F. *The Books and the Parchments: How We Got Our English Bible*. Revised and updated ed. Old Tappan, NJ: Fleming H. Revell, 1984.

Chrysostom, John. "OMIΛIA IB`." *Patrologia Graeca*. Paris: J.-P. Mingne, 1862.

Clark, Donald Lemen. *Rhetoric in Greco-Roman Education*. Morningside Heights, NY: Columbia University Press, 1957.

Cotterell, Peter and Max Turner. *Linguistics and Biblical Interpretation*. Downers Grove, IL: InterVarsity Press, 1989.

Dana, H. E. and Julius Mantey. *A Manual Grammar of the Greek New Testament*. Toronto: The Macmillan Company, 1957.

D'Angelo, Mary Rose. *Moses in the Letter to the Hebrews*. Society of Biblical Literature Dissertation Series. Missoula, MT: Scholars Press, 1979.

De Beaugrande, Robert-Alain and Wolfgang Dressler. *Introduction to Text Linguistics*. Longman Linguistics Library. New York: Longman, 1981.

Dodd, C. H. *The Parables of the Kingdom*. London: Nisbet & Co., 1935.

Dussaut, L. *Synopse Structurelle de l'Épître aux Hébreux: Approache d'Analyse Structurelle*. Paris: Les Editions du Cerf, 1981.

Ellingworth, Paul and Eugene Ellingworth. *A Translator's Handbook on the Letter to the Hebrews*. New York: United Bible Societies, 1983.

Ellis, E. Earle. *Prophecy and Hermeneutic in Early Christianity: New Testament Essays*. Grand Rapids, MI: Wm. B. Eerdmans, 1978.

——. *Paul's Use of the Old Testament*. Grand Rapids, MI: Baker Book House, 1981.

——. *The Old Testament in Early Christianity*. Tübingen: J. C. B. Mohr (Paul Siebeck), 1991.

Fee, Gordon. *New Testament Exegesis: A Handbook for Students and Pastors*. Philadelphia, PA: The Westminster Press, 1983.

Feld, Helmut. *Der Hebräerbrief Erträge der Forschung*. Darmstadt: Wissenschaftliche Buchgesel, 1985.

Filson, Floyd. *'Yesterday': A Study of Hebrews in Light of Chapter 13*. Studies in Biblical Theology. Naperville, IL: Alec R. Allenson, 1967.

Grässer, Erich. "Das Heil als Wort: Exegetische Erwägungen zu Hebr. 2,1-4." In *Neues Testament und Geschichte: Historisches Geschehen und Deutung im Neuen Testament*, ed. Heinrich Baltensweiler and Bo Reicke, 261-74. Tübingen: J. C. B. Mohr (Paul Siebeck), 1972.

Grimes, Joseph E. *The Thread of Discourse*. Paris: Mouton, 1975.

Gunkel, Hermann and Leopold Zscharnack, eds. *Religion in Geschichte und Gegenwart: Handwörterbuch für Theologie und Religionswissenschaft*. 2d ed. Tübingen: J. C. B. Mohr (Paul Siebeck), 1928. S.v. "Hebräerbrief," by F. Büchsel.

Guthrie, Donald. *New Testament Introduction.* Downers Grove, IL: Inter-varsity Press, 1976.

Guthrie, George H. "Exaltation Theology in Hebrews: A Discourse Analysis of the Function of Psalm 110:1 in Hebrews 1:3." Master's thesis, Trinity Evangelical Divinity School, 1989.

Hagen, Kenneth. *Hebrews Commenting from Erasmus to Bèza 1516-1598.* Beiträge zur Geschichte der Biblischen Exegese. Tübingin: J. C. B. Mohr (Paul Siebeck), 1981.

Halliday, Michael A. K. and Ruqaiya Hasan. *Cohesion in English.* London: Longman, 1976.

Hay, David M. *Glory at the Right Hand: Psalm 110 in Early Christianity.* Society of Biblical Literature Monograph Series, no. 18. Cambridge: University Press, 1980.

Hengel, Martin. *The Son of God.* Philadelphia: Fortress Press, 1976.

Hughes, Graham. *Hebrews and Hermeneutics: The Epistle to the Hebrews as a New Testament Example of Biblical Interpretation.* Cambridge: Cambridge University Press, 1979.

Jackson, Jared J., and Martin Kessler, eds. *Rhetorical Criticism: Essays in Honor of James Muilenburg.* Pittsburgh, PA: The Pickwick Press, 1974.

Käsemann, Ernst. *The Wandering People of God: An Investigation of the Letter to the Hebrews.* Translated by Roy A. Harrisville and Irving L. Sandberg. Minneapolis, MN: Augsburg, 1984.

Kennedy, George. *New Testament Interpretation Through Rhetorical Criticism.* Studies in Religion. Chapel Hill, NC: The University of North Carolina Press, 1984.

Kistemaker, Simon. *The Psalm Citations in the Epistle to the Hebrews.* Amsterdam: Soest, 1961.

Kosmala, Hans. *Hebräer, Essener, Christen: Studien zur Vorgeschichte der Fruhchristlichen Verkündigung.* Studia Post-Biblica. Leiden: Brill, 1959.

Kümmel, Werner Georg. *Introduction to the New Testament.* Translated by Howard Clark Kee. Nashville, TN: Abingdon, 1975.

Lausberg, Heinrich. *Hanbuch der Literarischen Rhetorik: Eine Grundlegung der Literaturwissenschaft.* München: Max Hueber, 1960.

Lindars, Barnabas. *New Testament Apologetic: The Doctrinal Significance of the Old Testament Quotations.* Philadelphia, PA: Westminster Press, 1961.

Longacre, Robert E. *An Anatomy of Speech Notions.* Lisse, Belgium: Peter de Ridder Press, 1976.

———. *Tagmemics.* Waco, TX: Word, 1985.

Longenecker, Richard N. *Biblical Exegesis in the Apostolic Period.* Grand Rapids, MI: Eerdmans, 1975.

Louw, J. P. *Semantics of New Testament Greek.* The Society of Biblical Literature Semeia Studies. Philadelphia, PA: Fortress Press, 1982.

Mack, Burton L. *Rhetoric and the New Testament.* Minneapolis, MN: Fortress Press, 1990.

Martin, Ralph. *Carmen Christi: Philippians ii.5-11 in Recent Interpretation and in the Setting of Early Christian Worship.* Cambridge: Cambridge University Press, 1967.

McCullough, J. C. "Hebrews and the Old Testament." Ph.D. diss., Queen's University Belfast, 1971.

Nauck, Wolfgang. "Zum Aufbau des Hebräerbriefes." In *Judentum Urchristentum Kirche: Festschrift für Joachim Jeremias,* ed. Walther Eltester. Berlin: Alfred Töpelmann, 1960.

Nestle, Eberhard and Erwin Nestle. *Novum Testamentum Graece.* 26th ed., ed. Kurt Aland and others. Stuttgart: Deutsche Bibelgesellschaft, 1979.

Nida, E. A., J. P. Louw, A. H. Snyman, and J. v. W. Cronje, eds. *Style and Discourse: With Special Reference to the Text of the Greek New Testament.* Cape Town: Bible Society, 1983.

Nissilä, Keijo. *Das Hohepriestmotiv in Hebräerbrief: Eine Exegetische Untersuchung.* Schriften der Finnischen exegetischen Gesellschaft. Helsinki: Oy Liiton Kirjapaino, 1979.

Perelmann, Chaim and L. Olbrechts-Tyteca. *The New Rhetoric: A Treatise on Argumentation.* Translated by John Wilkinson and Purcell Weaver. Notre Dame: Notre Dame University Press, 1969.

Russell, D. A., and M. Winterbottom, eds. *Ancient Literary Criticism: The Principal Texts in New Translations.* Oxford: Calrendon Press, 1972.

Sanders, Jack T. *The New Testament Christological Hymns: Their Historical and Religious Background.* Cambridge: The University Press, 1971.

Schierse, Franz Joseph. *Verheißung und Heilsvollendung: Zur theologischen Grundfrage des Hebräerbriefes.* Münchener Theologische Studien. Müchen: Karl Zink Verlag, 1954.

Schille, Gottfried. *Frühchristliche Hymnen.* 2d ed. Berlin: Evangelische Verlagsanstalt, 1965.

Schröger, F. *Der Verfasser des Hebräerbriefes als Schriftausleger.* Biblische Untersuchung. Regensburg: 1968.

Silva, Moisés. *Biblical Words and Their Meanings: An Introduction to Lexical Semantics.* Grand Rapids, MI: Zondervan, 1983.

Swetnam, James. *Jesus and Isaac: A Study of the Epistle to the Hebrews in the Light of the Aqedah.* Rome: Biblical Institute Press, 1981.

Thiselton, Anthony C. "Semantics and New Testament Interpretation." In *New Testament Interpretation: Essays on Principles and Methods,* ed. I. H. Marshall, 75-104. Grand Rapids, MI: Wm. B. Eerdmans, 1977.

Thyen, Hartwig. *Der Stil des jüdisch-hellenistischen Homilie.* Göttingen: Vandenhoeck & Ruprecht, 1955.

Turner, Nigel. *Syntax.* Vol. 3 in *A Grammar of New Testament Greek,* ed. James Hope Moulton. Edinburgh: T. & T. Clark, 1963.

Übelacker, Walter G. *Der Hebräerbrief als Appell: Untersuchungen zu exordium, narratio und postscriptum.* Coniectanea Biblica, New Testament Series. Stockholm, Sweden: Almqvist & Wiksell, 1989.

Vaganay, Léon. "Le Plan de L'Épître aux Hébreux." In *Mémorial Lagrange,* ed., L.-H. Vincent, 269-77. Paris: J. Gabalda, 1940.

Van Dijk, Teun. *Text and Context.* New York: Longman, 1977.

Vanhoye, Albert. *La structure littéraire de l'Épître aux Hébreux.* 2d ed. Paris: Desclée de Brouwer, 1976.

———. *Épître aux Hébreux: Texte Grec Structuré.* Rome: Institut Biblique Pontifical, 1967.

Volkmann, Richard. *Die Rhetorik der Griechen und Römer in Systematischer übersicht.* Leipzig: B. G. Teubner, 1885.

Von Soden, Hermann F. *Urchristliche Literaturgeschichte: die Schriften des Neuen Testaments.* Berlin: Alexander Duncker, 1905.

Watson, Duane Frederick. *Invention, Arrangement, and Style: Rhetorical Criticism of Jude and 2 Peter.* SBL Dissertation Series. Atlanta, GA: Scholars Press, 1988.

Williamson, Ronald. *Philo and the Epistle to the Hebrews.* Leiden: E. J. Brill, 1970.

Wright, Addison G. *Midrash: The Literary Genre.* New York: Alba House, 1967.

Zimmermann, H. *Das Bekenntnis der Hoffnung: Tradition und Redaktion im Hebräerbrief.* Köln: Peter Hanstein Verlag, 1977.

Journal Articles

Andriessen, P. C. B. "La Teneur Judeo-Chretienne de HE 1:6 et 2:14b-3:2." *Novum Testamentum* 18 (April 1976): 293-313.
Attridge, H. W. "'Let Us Strive to Enter that Rest': the Logic of Hebrews 4:1-11." *Harvard Theological Review* 73 (1980): 279-88.
Auffret, P. "Note sur la structure littéraire d'Hb ii.1-4." *New Testament Studies* 25 (February 1979): 166-79.
———. "Essai sur la structure littéraire et l'interprétation d'Hébreux 3,1-6." *New Testament Studies* 26 (March 1980): 380-96.
Betz, Hans-Dieter. "The Literary Composition and Function of Paul's Letter to the Galatians." *New Testament Studies* 21 (1975): 353-79.
Black, David A. "Hebrews 1:1-4: A Study in Discourse Analysis." *Westminster Theological Journal* 49 (1987): 175-94.
———. "A Note on the Structure of Hebrews 12:1-2." *Biblica* 68 (1987): 543-51.
———. "The Problem of the Literary Structure of Hebrews: An Evaluation and a Proposal." *Grace Theological Journal* 7 (1986):163-77.
Borchert, G. L. "A Superior Book: Hebrews." *Review and Expositor* 82 (1985): 319-32.
Bristol, L. O. "Primitive Christian Preaching and the Epistle to the Hebrews." *Journal of Biblical Literature* 68 (1949): 89-97.
Bruce, F. F. "'To the Hebrews' or 'To the Essenes'?" *New Testament Studies* 9 (1962-1963): 217-32.
———. "The Kerygma of Hebrews." *Interpretation* 23 (January 1969): 3-19.
———. "The Structure and Argument of Hebrews." *Southwestern Journal of Theology* 28 (1985): 6-12.
Büchel, C. "Der Hebräerbrief und das Alte Testament." *Theologische Studien und Kritiken* (1906): 338.
Caird, G. B. "The Exegetical Method of the Epistle to the Hebrews." *Canadian Journal of Theology* 5 (1959): 44-51.
Clements, R. E. "The Use of the Old Testament in Hebrews." *Southwestern Journal of Theology* 28 (1985): 36-45.
Cohn-Sherbok, Dan. "Paul and Rabbinic Exegesis." *Scottish Journal of Theology* 35 (1982): 117-32.
Combrink, H. J. B. "Some Thoughts on the OT Citations in the Epistle to the Hebrews." *Neotestamentica* 5 (1971): 22-36.
Cockerill, Gareth Lee. "Heb. 1:1-14, 1 Clem. 36:1-6 and the High Priest Title." *Journal of Biblical Literature* 97 (1978): 437-40.
Cosby, Michael R. "The Rhetorical Composition of Hebrews 11." *Journal of Biblical Literature* 107 (1988): 250-70.
Daube, D. "Rabbinic Methods of Interpretation and Hellenistic Rhetoric." *Hebrew Union College Annual* 22 (1949): 239-64.
Descamps, A. "La structure de l'Épître aux Hébreux." *Revue Diocésaine de Tournai* 9 (1954): 251-58, 333-38.
Ellingworth, P. "Jesus and the Universe in Hebrews." *Evangelical Quarterly* 58 (1986): 337-50.
Ellis, E. Earle. "Isaiah in the New Testament." *Southwestern Journal of Theology.* 34 (1991): 31-35.
Feuillet, A. "Une triple préparation du sacerdoce du Christ dans l'Ancien Testament (Melchisédec, le Messie du Ps 110, le Serviteur d'Is 53). Introduction à la doctrine sacerdotale de l'Épître aux Hébreux." *Divinitas* 28 (1984): 103-36.
Fitzmyer, J. A. "'Now this Melchizedek' (Heb. 7:1)." *Catholic Biblical Quarterly* 25 (1963): 305-21.

———. "The Use of the Explicit Old Testament Quotations in the Qumran Literature and in the New Testament." *New Testament Studies* 7 (1961): 297-333.

Frankowski, Janusz. "Early Christian Hymns Recorded in the New Testament: A Reconsideration of the Question in the Light of Heb. 1:3." *Biblische Zeitschrift* 27 (1983): 183-94.

George, Howard. "Hebrews and OT Quotations." *Novum Testamentum* 10 (1968): 208-16.

Glasson, T. F. "Plurality of Divine Persons and the Quotations in Hebrews i.6ff." *New Testament Studies* 12 (March 1966): 270-72.

Gourgues, M. "Remarques sur la 'structure centralé de l'Épître aux Hébreux. D l'occasion d'une réédition." *Review Biblique* 84 (1977): 26-37.

Grässer, Erich. "Der Hebräerbrief 1938-1963." *Theologische Rundschau* 30 (1964): 138-236.

———. "Das wandernde Gottesvolk. Zum Basismotiv des Hebräerbriefes." *Zeitschrift für die neutestamentliche Wissenschaft* 77 (1986): 160-79.

———. "Mose und Jesus. Zur Zuslegung von Hebr 3:1-6." *Zeitschrift für die neutestamentliche Wissenschaft* 75 (1984): 2-23.

Gyllenberg, Rafael. "Die Komposition des Hebräerbriefs." *Svensk Exegetisk Årsbok* 22 (1957-58): 137-47.

Haering, Theodore. "Gedankengang und Grundgedanken des Hebräerbriefs," *Zeitschrift für die neutestamentliche Wissenschaft* 18 (1917-18): 145-64.

Harris, Murray J. "The Translation and Significance of ὁ θεός in Hebrews 1:8-9." *Tyndale Bulletin* 36 (1985): 129-62.

Hughes, P. E. "The Christology of Hebrews." *Southwestern Journal of Theology* 28 (1985): 19-27.

Jewett, Robert. "Romans as an Ambassadorial Letter." *Interpretation* 36 (1982): 5-20.

Katz, P. "The Quotations from Deuteronomy in Hebrews." *Zeitschrift für die neuetestamentliche Wissenschaft* 49 (1958): 213-23.

Koops, R. "Chains of Contrasts in Hebrews 1" *Biblical Translator* 34 (February 1983): 220-25.

Kuss, O. "Über einige neuere Beiträge zur Exegese des Hebräerbriefes." *Theologie und Glaube* 42 (1952): 186-204.

Lane, William. "Hebrews: A Sermon in Search of a Setting." *Southwestern Journal of Theology* 28 (1985): 13-18.

Le Déaut, R. "A propos d'une définition du midrash." *Biblica* 50 (1969): 395-413.

Lindars, Barnabas. "The Rhetorical Structure of Hebrews." *New Testament Studies* 35 (1989): 382-406.

Loader, W. R. G. "Christ at the Right Hand: Psalm 110:1 in the New Testament." *New Testament Studies* 24 (1978): 199-217.

Lohmann, T. "Zur Heilsgeschichte des Hebräerbriefes." *Orientalische Literaturzeitung* 79 (1984): 117-25.

Lombard, H. A. "Κατάπαυσις in the Letter to the Hebrews." *Neotestamentica* 5 (1971): 60-71.

MacNamera, Martin. "Some Issues and Recent Writings on Judaism and the NT." *Irish Biblical Studies* 9 (1987): 136-49.

McCullough, J. C. "Some Recent Developments in Research on the Epistle to the Hebrews." *Irish Biblical Studies* 2 (July 1980): 141-65.

———. "Some Recent Developments in Research on the Epistle to the Hebrews: II." *Irish Biblical Studies* 3 (1981): 28-43.

———. "The Old Testament Quotations in Hebrews." *New Testament Studies* 26 (1979-80): 363-79.

McGehee, M. "Hebrews: The Letter Which is not a Letter." *Bib Today* 24 (1986): 213-16.

Meier, J. P. "Structure and Theology in Heb. 1,1-14." *Biblica* 66 (1985): 168-89.

———. "Symmetry and Theology in the Old Testament Citations of Heb. 1,5-14." *Biblica* 66 (1985): 504-33.

Miller, M. P. "Targum, Midrash and the Use of the Old Testament in the New Testament." *Journal for the Study of Judaism* 2 (1970): 29-82.

Muilenberg, James. "Form Criticism and Beyond." *Journal of Biblical Literature* 88 (1969): 1-18.

Neeley, Linda Lloyd. "A Discourse Analysis of Hebrews." *Occasional Papers in Translation and Textlinguistics* 3-4 (1987): 1-146.

Oberholtzer, T. K. "The Warning Passages in Hebrews. Part 1 (of 5 parts): The Eschatological Salvation of Hebrews 1:5-2:5." *Bibliotheca Sacra* 145 (1988): 83-97.

Olson, S. N. "Wandering but Not Lost." *Word World* 5 (1985): 426-33.

Omanson, R. L. "A Superior Covenant: Hebrews 8:1-10:18." *Review and Expositor* 82 (1985): 361-73.

Parunack, H. Van Dyke. "Transitional Techniques in the Bible." *Journal of Biblical Literature* 102 (1983): 525-48.

Paul, M. J. "The Order of Melchizedek (Ps 110:4 and Heb 7:3)." *Westminster Theological Journal* 49 (1987): 195-211.

Rice, G. E. "The Chiastic Structure of the Central Section of the Epistle to the Hebrews." *Andrews University Seminary Studies* 19 (1981): 243-46.

Robinson, D. W. B. "The Literary Structure of Heb. 1:1-4." *Australian Journal of Biblical Archaeology* 2 (January 1972): 178-86.

Strobel, August. "Die Psalmengrundlage der Gethsemane-Parallele Hbr. 5,7ff." *Zeitschrift für die neutestamentliche Wissenshaft* 45 (1954): 252-66.

Swetnam, James. "Form and Content in Hebrews 1-6." *Biblica* 53 (1972): 368-85.

———. "Form and Content in Hebrews 7-13." *Biblica* 55 (1974): 333-48.

———. "On the Literary Genre of the 'Epistle' to the Hebrews." *Novum Testamentum* 11 (1969): 261-69.

———. Review of *Chiastic Analysis of the Epistle to the Hebrews* by John Bligh. In *Catholic Biblical Quarterly* 29 (1967): 134.

Thien, F. "Analyse de L'Épître aux Hébreux." *Revue Biblique* 11 (1902): 74-86.

Thomas, K. J. "The Old Testament Citations in Hebrews." *New Testament Studies* 11 (1965): 303-25.

Thompson, J. W. "The Structure and Purpose of the Catena in Heb. 1:5-13." *Catholic Biblical Quarterly* 38 (March 1976): 352-63.

———. "The Conceptual Background and Purpose of the Midrash in Heb. 7." *Novum Testamentum* 19 (1977): 209-23.

Thornton, T. C. G. Review of *La structure littéraire de l'Épître aux Hébreux* by Albert Vanhoye. *Journal of Theological Studies* 15 (1964): 137-41.

Thurston, R. W. "Philo and the Epistle to the Hebrews." *Evangelical Quarterly* 58 (1986): 133-43.

Toussaint, S. D. "The Eschatology of the Warning Passages in the Book of Hebrews." *Grace Theological Journal* 3 (January 1982): 67-80.

Ulrichsen, Jarl Henning. "Διαφορώτερον in Hebr. 1,4. Christus als Träger des Gottesnamens." *Studia Theologica* 38 (1984): 65-75.

Van der Ploeg, J. "L'exégèse de l'Ancien Testament dans l'Épître aux Hébreux." *Revue Biblique* 54 (1947): 187-228.

Vanhoye, Albert. "De Sessione Caelesti." *Epistola ad Verbum Domini* 44 (1966): 131-34.

———. "Discussions sur la structure de l'Épître Hébreux." *Biblica* 55 (1974): 349-80.

———. "Trois Ouvarages récent sur l'Épître aux Hébreux." *Biblica* 52 (January 1971): 62-71.

———. "Longue marche ou accès tout proche? Le context biblique de Hébreux 3,7-4,11." *Biblica* 49 (January 1968): 9-26.

———. "Literarische Struktur und theologische Botschaft des Hebräerbriefs (1. Teil)." *Studien für die Neue Testament Umwelt* 4 (1979): 119-47.

———. "Literarische Struktur und theologische Botschaft des Hebräerbriefs (2. Teil)." *Studien für die Neue Testament Umwelt* 5 (1980): 18-49.

Williamson, R. "The Incarnation of the Logos in Hebrews." *Expository Times* 95 (1983): 4-8.

Wuellner, Wilhelm. "Paul's Rhetoric of Argumentation in Romans." *Catholic Biblical Quarterly* 38 (1976): 330-51.

———. "Where is Rhetorical Criticism Taking Us?" *Catholic Biblical Quarterly* 49 (1987): 449-55.

AUTHOR INDEX

SUBJECT INDEX

George Guthrie (Ph.D., Southwestern Baptist Theological Seminary) is associate professor of Christian studies at Union University. He is the coauthor (with J. Scott Duvall) of Biblical Greek Exegesis.